Attic Kylix, 6th Cent. B.C. *(Courtesy Director of Antiquities, Cyprus Museum)*

PAPHOS
LAND OF APHRODITE

Written by
RENOS G. LAVITHIS

Supervision
Dr. Stavros Panteli

Edited by
Anna Lavithis

INTERWORLD
PUBLICATIONS

PAPHOS
Land of Aphrodite

A South Western Cyprus Tourist Guide

Published by
INTERWORLD PUBLICATIONS
12 The Fairway, New Barnet
Herts. EN5 1HN, London-England
Tel. 081-449 5938

CYPRUS AGENTS
14-16 King Constantine 12th Avenue
Paphos — Tel. 235056

• First Published in 1983
• Second Revised Edition 1984
• Reprint in 1986
• Third Revised Edition 1987
• Reprint in 1989
• Fourth Revised Edition 1990

ISBN 0 948853 14 X

NOTICE

Every precaution has been taken to ensure accuracy of the information contained in this book but the publishers accept no responsibility for errors or omissions nor for statements in advertisements.

CONTENTS

PLEASE NOTE
TELEPHONE NUMBERS CHANGED

At the time of going to press all numbers to Paphos have changed. The code instead of being 061 now becomes 06 and the digital 2 is added in front of all existing numbers.

All photographs (except those credited individually have been taken by the author – No reproduction is allowed.

FOREWORD FROM THE AUTHOR

Paphos is alive again. After many hundreds of years of neglect and isolation, is now fully revitalised with visitors from all over Europe. This time you are not coming to pay homage to Aphrodite and participate in the annual celebrations; you are coming to admire the past, to enjoy the present and explore the beautiful and contrasting coast and countryside.

When as a youngster I used to wonder around the empty spaces of Kato Paphos pretending to be an amateur archaeologist and sitting for hours watching the few barges loading carrobs or almonds onto a lonely boat offshore, or unloading other goods, never did I imagine that the place one day would be buzzing with life, with an International Airport, only four hours away from London. Now the barges have gone and no commercial boats call to Paphos, but the small idyllic harbour is full of activity with fishing boats and pleasure boats.

This sudden and rapid expansion is good up to a point and I hope that the wisdom which prevailed so far will continue to restrict unscrupulous property developments, although, I must admit some isolated but very bad decisions were taken recently.

The success of the 1983 edition and the second enlarged edition of 1984 has allowed us to expand to the third edition with a special section about the place and the Cult of Aphrodite.

This Fourth Edition has minor changes and a new page on accommodation to cater for the rapid expansion in this field.

I would like to express my heartfelt thanks to the following:
My associate Dr. Stavros Panteli for all his help and editing, my wife Anna for all her encouragement; Mr. Karlis Agrotis, Mr. Stass Paraskos, Professor George Eliades, the directors and staff of the Cyprus Museum and Paphos Museum, the directors and staff of the Cyprus Tourism Organisation, Mr. Stephanos Theodorou, Mr. Costas K. Georgiou, Dr. C. Theophanides, Mr. Fivos Roussis, Mr. Michael Mavroudis and Dr. Demetris Michaelides.

Have a wonderful time in Paphos.

Renos G. Lavithis

Dedicated to my Daughter Niki K. Lavithis

CHAPTER 1

THE HISTORY OF PAPHOS

State of Paphos *(Courtesy Director of Antiquities, Cyprus Museum)*

Paphos is the south-western corner of Cyprus and by nature is separated from the rest of the island by mountains. The main connection with the other towns is by the road to Limassol which runs in some places along the coast and goes inland from the Rock of Aphrodite (Petra tou Romiou), climbing up a steep mountain, resembling a scene from a western film.

However, there have been times in the past when Paphos was more or less isolated from the rest of the island and developed its own identity, although communication was possible by land and sea. The fleets of the Greeks, Romans and, in later times, the Crusaders used Paphos as the natural harbour for rest and supplies: thus Paphos flourished through this trade and developed importance.

Although part of Paphos' history blends with the fortunes and misfortunes of the whole island, there are events which happened locally; these are worth mentioning, as they help the reader to understand Paphos, which is thought of as a living museum.

It is worthy of note that Paphos was important in the ancient Greek world and mentioned in the poems of Homer. This is mainly due to the fact that it was the centre for the worship of Aphrodite.

THE EARLY YEARS

Traces of human life in Paphos going back as far as the Neolithic and Chalcolithic periods around the middle of the 7th millenium BC, have been found in many places, the most important being at the villages of Lemba, Yialia and Souskiou.

BRONZE (OR COPPER) AGE 2500 — 1500 BC

As in the rest of Cyprus, Paphos has seen a tremendous change at various times with settlers coming over from Greece, mainly Achaeans and Mycenean Greeks.

1500 — 1000 BC

Migration from the Greek cities continued and the kingdoms of Paphos (Paleapaphos) which eventually became the centre for the religion of Aphrodite (founded by Agapenor) and Marion were established, with other settlements at Maa-Paleokastron, Akamas, and around the harbour of Paphos.

The Greek settlements remained well into the year 1000 BC and the settlers introduced a new way of life, which is still strongly in evidence today.

1000 — 700 BC

Phoenicians settled in parts of Cyprus.

As with the whole of the eastern Mediterranean Paphos suffered decline and many natural disasters. However, Paleapaphos retained its importance.

Cyprus under the influence of Assyrian kings.

700 — 500 BC

Paphos re-emerged at this time as a commercial centre and economic relations were established, mainly with Assyria and Egypt. The Palaces of Nineveh of the Assyrian King

LEFT:L nestone female idol from Lemba. Right: Stealife idol: both from Chalcolithic period *(Courtesy Director of Antiquities, Cyprus Museum).*

Assharaddon were built with timber supplied by Eteandros, the King of Paphos. Short Egyptian rule of the island. In 545 the Cypriot kings submitted to the rule of Persia thus Cyprus became a centre of conflict between Greece & Persia as the Greeks considered Cyprus as part of the Greek world.

4TH AND 3RD CENTURIES BC

The wars between Greece and Persia entered a new phase with the emergence of Alexander the Great and his drive against the Persian might.

Paphos took positive action against the Persian rulers of Cyprus and supplied Alexander The Great with ships and men during the occupation and capture of Tyre. The mint of Paphos produced and supplied money to help the war effort. According to archaeological evidence Nea Paphos, or Kato Paphos (the area in and around the harbour) was established as the commercial and administrative centre by   King Nicocles. This coincided with the destruction of Marion (Polis) in 312 BC, during the wars between the Antiochus of Asia Minor and Ptolemy of Egypt. The Ptolemy of Egypt was the victor and became the ruler of Cyprus. King Nicocles defended Paphos but eventually he was defeated. Legend says that he committed suicide with all the Royal Family.

294 — 58 BC

The Ptolemaic rulers of Egypt, after their victory, took control of Paphos and the whole of Cyprus. The mint continued to expand and Nea Paphos became a very important centre, being accepted as the commercial and administrative centre of Cyprus.

Arts and commerce continued to flourish and Paphos became a very important cultural centre. The tale-writer Alexandros, the historian Istros and the poet Sopartos came to be some of the most famous men of the time.

58 BC

The Romans conquered Cyprus and took Paphos. A proconsul was appointed in Nea Paphos. The first administrator was called Cato.

58 BC-330 AD

During the Roman period Paphos remained the capital of Cyprus, both commercially and culturally. Cicero, the famous Roman orator, was a proconsul in Paphos from 51 to 50 BC. The Greek language retained its importance as mosaics and coins show.

There was economic and political stability.

15AD

Paphos, which by this time had reached the height of its importance under the Emperor Octavianus Augustus, was destroyed by a devastating earthquake. The Emperor supervised the re-building of the town and also the Temple of Aphrodite at Paleapaphos. Paphos was also called the "Claudian Flavian Paphos" — the sacred metropolis of Cities of Cyprus.

45/46 AD

Paphos was involed in the new Christian religion. The Apostles St. Paul, St. Mark and St. Barnabas reached Paphos during their

From left to right: Marble statue of Aphrodite from Nea Paphos — Roman period. Marble statue of Asklepios from Nea Paphos — 2nd Cent. A.D. Ivory mirror handle from Paleapaphos — 12th Cent. B.C. Funerary relief stele of Aristila from Marion — 420 B.C. *(Courtesy Director of Antiquities, Cyprus Museum)*

visit to Cyprus. It was here that one of the most important incidents happened during the post-Christ period. Elymas, a prominent member of the Jewish community and advisor to the Governor, was alarmed by the interest being shown by the Roman Governor and tried to keep him away from St. Paul. St. Paul was punished by being tied to a column and given 39 lashes. In his anger St. Paul punished Elymas by blinding him. The Roman Governor was so impressed by St. Paul's teachings that he became the first Roman of high rank to become a Christian. The incident has no historical proof and is believed by some to be more fiction than fact, although it is true that St. Paul did succeed in converting the Roman Governor to Christianity. The Governor's name was Sergius Paulus. Many of the local people then followed the Governor's example and converted to Christianity. From this point Paphos became an important centre for Christian worship. As in all the other parts of the Roman Empire, Christianity became illegal and persecution followed over the next decades by Roman Emperors. Worship was caried out in secret in catacombs and other places such as Ayia Solomoni, Ayios Lambrianos and The Tombs of The Kings.

3RD AND 4TH CENTURIES

Strong earthquakes in 332 and 342 AD practically destroyed Nea Paphos, which then entered into decline. Salamis (in Famagusta) then became the capital of Cyprus. Cyprus became part of the new Byzantine Empire (or the Eastern Roman Empire as it was first called) and Christianity was the main religion.

379-395

Severe penalties were imposed by the Byzantine Emperors to the worshippers of Aphrodite and those making sacrifices to idols.

648-963

Further suffering and destruction followed with successive Arab invasions, mainly by General Abdul Halign Kaif. Many monuments were almost totally destroyed and many treasures and slaves were taken away. Inhabitants fled from the port area and settled on the high ground, which is now the modern town of Ktima

965

The Arab raids were brought to an end by the Byzantine Emperor Nicephorus Phokas and peace followed.

11TH AND 12TH CENTURIES

Paphos saw normal life return to the area and there were periods of prosperity; this time was also the beginning of the Crusades. Many pilgrims landed in Paphos on their way to the Holy Land for rest and supplies. Some of them decided to stay and settle in Paphos, including the Duke of Savoy, Armendeus, and Eric III — the King of Denmark — who died here. By this time the Latins had become very powerful and influential.

1192-1489

This was the period when Cyprus was occupied by the Lusignans. Paphos was a very important commercial port and many wealthy Greeks and Franks stayed here. There emerged a struggle between the local Orthodox Christians and the Catholic Lusignans. The Latin Bishops established their seat in Paphos and the Greek Orthodox Bishop was exiled to the small town of Arsinoe (the new name of Marion). The Lusignans established a Royal Domain and introduced their feudal system. All the land was given to the rich families and the peasants were forced to work in the fields. Sugar cane was one of the major products.

1372

Paphos became the centre of hostilities between the Lusignans and the Genoese, who were trying to occupy parts of Cyprus. A Cypriot chronicler called Leontius Machaeras describes:

"The Genoese called to their assistance many men of bad character. And there gathered together Bulgarians, Greeks and Tartars close upon 2000 men and they went and took the castle of Paphos...........when the news of what the Genoese had done reached the capital (Nicosia), the king ordered that the Prince of Antioch should be made commander. He chose 1000 good fighting men and went to Paphos on Sunday the 3rd of July 1372. Early in the morning, the said Prince went to the tower of Paphos and began the attack. The enemy went into their galleys and came out from time to time and fought with him. The battle lasted for hours but to no avail because the Genoese had great help from the Bulgarians. The Prince's company did vast damage to the galleys but his expedition failed. The Prince went away and returned to Nicosia. And when the captains of the galleys learned that the Prince and his army had returned to Nicosia, they landed a company of men to collect slaves and they went and made captives in all the districts and took many men, women and children and they took away much food and cattle."

Paphos remained under Genoese rule until March of 1373 when hostilities ended and an armistice was declared between the Lusignans and Genoese in the whole of Cyprus.

1481

Felix Faber, a traveller, described Paphos: *"No longer a city but a miserable village built over ruins. The harbour being abandoned and ships only entering it when forced to do so, as was our fate ...."*

1489-1571 AD - VENETIAN PERIOD

This was the period of Venetian occupation in Cyprus. Paphos became a more important port for supplying the Venetian fleet. A garrison was stationed near the harbour.

1571-1878

Cyprus entered a new era of occupation by the Ottoman Turks. Nicosia and Famagusta, which were nearer to Turkey, became more important places and Paphos was in continuing decline with the exception of certain agricultural areas which were allowed to keep going. Kato Paphos practically became a ghost town and **Ktima** (the modern city) emerged as the centre for administration. Dr. L. Ross said in 1845 - *Paphos port is a deserted, ugly, largely ruined place with a few inhabitants".*

1821

Following the Greek revolution in mainland Greece the Turkish administration in Cyprus carried out a purge which extended to Paphos and ` Bishop Chrysanthos, together with other prominent citizens, was executed.

1878

A new chapter opened in Cyprus' history. The British took over the occupation of the island from the Turks. Paphos, being situated far away from the administrative centres of Nicosia and Larnaca, remained a small town but grew in beauty with new administration buildings, a library, schools and green gardens and parks.

1960

After its struggle for independence Cyprus became a free nation and a member of the United Nations. Paphos gained fame once again since the first President of the Republic and world statesman, the late Archbishop Makarios, was born in the mountain village of Panayia   One of his aims was to bring Paphos closer to the rest of the island with new roads, small industries, expansion of agriculture and growth of the tourist industry. The expansion, which was halted briefly during the Turkish invasion of Cyprus in 1974, continued and the new refugees (since the August 1974 invasion) who came from the occupied north of Cyprus, together with the local people put all their energy and commercial expertise to work in new developments, new hotels and new industries.

Now that you have learned a little about the history oif Paphos through the ages, and although archaeology is not often the interest of most, it might help you to appreciate this lovely, fascinating place and the people, who will provide every service so that you can have an enjoyable holiday.

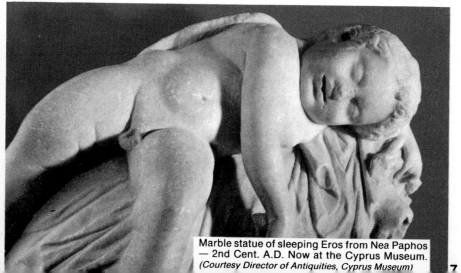

Marble statue of sleeping Eros from Nea Paphos
— 2nd Cent. A.D. Now at the Cyprus Museum.
(Courtesy Director of Antiquities, Cyprus Museum)

7

CHAPTER 2
Part One:
KTIMA (Paphos Town)

The Bishopric Palace and Ayios Theodoros   The Fruit Market

Today Paphos includes two main towns. The modern town of Ktima, built on a rocky plateau overlooking the sea, which is the capital of the district; and Kato Paphos (Lower Paphos) which is the ancient city around the harbour (this area was known as Nea Paphos), plus the new city built to the east the harbour with hotels, apartment blocks, restaurants, etc. Please note that the whole area is called Paphos.

KTIMA(PAPHOS)

This town was first established by the fleeing inhabitants of Nea Paphos during the first Arab raids and at that time it became an agricultural centre with large farms However, there is evidence that people were living here prior to this, as discovered tombs have shown. The word Ktima means property. During the Frankish period of the Lusignans many people came to settle here among the beautiful orchids. The town's main function and the reason for its importance is its commercial, cultural and administrative centre for the Paphos district. In the narrow streets of the shopping centre one can buy practically everything and, although most of the shops do not have vast window displays, one should not hesitate to go inside and inquire about a particular purchase. Although in most cases prices are displayed, one can enter into the

Kennedy Square

The Gymnasium (higher education building).

art of bargaining if one so wishes and money can be saved! The fruit and vegetable market is to be found at the end of Makarios III Avenue. The market is covered and here one can buy almost anything one wishes to eat.

PLACES OF INTEREST IN KTIMA

There are no major archaeological sites to visit in Ktima but there are, nevertheless, some very interesting places. In several parts of the town tombs of various periods have been discovered with burial finds, none though remains to be seen except one tomb which can be seen at the Ethnographical Museum (see below).

Hellenospellios: This locality situated near the old Chiftlik of Basilikon at the north east of the town, is unknown even to many locals. Interesting rock-hewn tombs of Hellenistic-Roman years were found here; of unique type in Cyprus, similar to others found in North Africa, Palestine and Syria. It is believed they were later used by early Christians as tombs and chapels.

Private Ethnographical Museum of Professor G. S. Eliades

This museum is situated at No 1 Exo Vrysis Street, between Palamas Square and the Bishopric Palace. There is a fine collection of bygones of Cyprus, from the Neolithic period to today. They are delightfully displayed in a charming house full of character both interior and exterior. A rock cut tomb is open to the public and situated at the far end of an open courtyard. Rooms show the way peasants used to live, their clothes, etc. and there is a bedroom, kitchen and working room. The museum is open daily and again, well worth visiting.

Entrance fee and conducted tours, Tel. (061) 32010.

Akropolis Square

This square , part of which is a restaurant and cafeteria/club, is next to the Bishopric of Paphos and sitting there gives the visitor a panoramic view of the Kato Paphos area with the harbour, lighthouse, the modern buildings and the coastline.

Palamas Square

This small square at the southern end of the Public Garden has a bust of the famous modern Greek poet Kostis Palamas. In the middle of the square there is a cupid temple with a small statuette inside, (a copy of "The Sleeping Eros".) The original was found in Paphos and is now on display in the Nicosia Musuem.

28th October Square

This is a square every visitor passes through. One cannot miss it, since in the centre there is single high column of Corinthian style erected as a monument to the Greek heroes of the Second World War. On the north side of the square stand the Elementary School, the Gymnasium and the entrance to the stadium, all built in Neoclassical style. On other sides of the square are the Public Library and The Town Hall, again all built in Neoclassical style. The idea of the square and the surrounding gardens was that of a progressive mayor of Paphos, Galatopoullos, a politician and poet who died in 1953 at an early age. The Police Station, which is on the opposite side of the square is of Typical British Colonial architectural style.

Public Gardens

Close to the Palamas and 28th October Squares are the Public Gardens, small but restful with green trees, bushes and flowers. There is a tennis court, a cafeteria, public toilets and for those who have small children, an ideal playground.

One of the rooms of the Ethnographical Museum.

A scene from the Public Market

The Public Market

This is situated just after the far end of Makarios III Avenue, in the heart of the main shopping area. In the market you can obtain fresh fruit & vegetables, fish and meat. Every Saturday morning many villagers bring their own fruit & vegetables which they display in the surrounding narrow streets. The atmosphere is very pleasant and for those staying in self-catering accommodation it is a golden opportunity to obtain extra bargains especially nearer to closing time which is 1pm.

Kostis Palamas Square: It was established in 1951 by the Mayor Galatopoullos in memory of the famous Greek Poet Palamas who's bust, as seen here in front of the public gardens, was the work of the sculptor Tombros. Every March a Palamas festival of poetry takes place.

10

A typical shop in the old market area of Paphos (Ktima Town).

The Cupid Temple at Palamas Square. Inside there is a copy of the famous statuette of the sleeping Eros.

The Byzantine Museum

This interesting Museum showing items of the Byzantine Period with many religious objects as Icons, wood carvings etc., is now situated in No. 26, 25th March Street, behind the Public Gardens. Tel. (061) 32466.

Please note: This museum will be shortly incorporated with the Bishopric Palace to form a new museum of BYZANTINE ART.

The Bishopric Palace

This beautifully designed building is the seat the Bishop of Paphos and is near Akropo Square, next to the church of Ayios Theodore There is a collection of rare manuscripts, ico and other religious objects. A special appoin ment is required.

1 Illysion St., Tel. (061) 32092/32361.

Public Library

This library to the west side of 28th Octob Square has a small but interesting collection books in Greek, English and some in Fren related to history, poetry and literature.
Open daily. Tel. (061) 32010.

Above left: An icon from the Byzantine Museum collection. *Above right:* the Library.
Below: The higher education buildings, situated t the north of the Public Gardens.

HE PAPHOS DISTRICT USEUM

The Museum is situated at the far end of oforos George Grivas Dhigheni towards roskipos. It is a small museum housed in a odern building but it has a very fine collection vering the entire Paphos district from as far ck as the Neolithic period, through the onze Age, Hellenistic, Roman and Byzantine nes. The museum is open daily but check for ening hours from the hotel or the tourist formation office.

ere are at present 4 rooms and plans for tensions. The collection is arranged chronogically. The 1st room is dedicated to the eolithic and Bronze Age periods. The 2nd to e Iron Age and the Classical period and shows tues, tombstones, inscriptions etc. In the 3rd om there are objects from the Hellenistic and oman period. These include statues *(including o Venuses)*, lamps, terracotta figurines etc.

arther exhibits are spread to rooms 4 and 5 (the th just recently completed) and include yzantine and Medieval Paphos.
el. (06) 232554.

Above and below: Exhibits from The Paphos District Museum which is worth visiting.

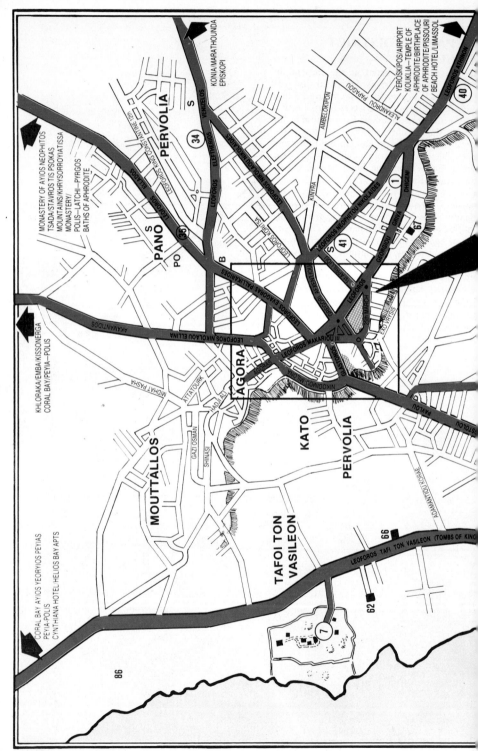

14

CENTRE OF PAPHOS TOWN

KATO PAPHOS

MUSEUMS & COLLECTIONS
(1) ARCHAEOLOGICAL MUSEUM
(2) PRIVATE ETHNOGRAPHICAL MUSEUM
(3) BYZANTINE M USEUM
(4) BISHOPRIC PALACE COLLECTION
(Soon to be moved to Bishopric Palace)
(5) PUBLIC LIBRARY
(6) ART GALLERY

MAIN ARCHAEOLOGICAL SITES
(see also special maps)
(7) TOMBS OF KINGS
(8) NORTH WESTERN GATE
(9) THE ODEON
(10) THE HOUSE OF DIONYSOS
(11) THE HOUSE OF AEONOS
(12) THE HOUSE OF ORPHEUS
(13) THE HOUSE OF THESEUS
(14) BYZANTINE CASTLE
(15) MEDIEVAL CASTLE
(16) AYIA SOLOMONI CATACOMBS
(17) GOTHIC CATHEDRAL & ST. PAUL'S
PILLAR
(18) BASILICA
(19) FABRICA HILL
(20) SANCTUARY OF APOLLO HYLATES

(21) FRANKISH BATHS
(22) TURKISH BATHS
(23) EASTERN NEKROPOLIS
(New finds of Tombs)

CHURCHES & OTHER PLACES
(24) AYIOS THEODOROS
(25) AYIOS IOANNIS
(26) AYIOS KENDEAS
(27) AYIA THEOSKEPASTI
(28) KHRYSOPOLITISSA CHURCH
(AYIA KYRIAKI)
(29) AYIOS ANTONIOS (Anglican Church)
(30) OLD AYIA SOPHIA (Mosque)

PUBLIC & OTHER PLACES
(31) TOURIST INFORMATION OFFICE
(32) CYPRUS AIRWAYS
(33) PERVOLA BUS STATION
(34) YOUTH HOSTEL
(35) NICOLOMIDEN SCHOOL
(36) POLICE HEADQUARTERS
(37) GENERAL POST OFFICE
(38) LAW COURT, DISTRICT OFFICE,
LAND REGISTRY OFFICE

(39) TELEGRAPHIC OFFICE
(40) FIRE BRIGADE
(41) GENERAL HOSPITAL
(42) TOWN HALL
(43) 28th OCTOBER SQUARE
(44) PALAMAS SQUARE
(45) SLEEPING EROS
(46) KENNEDY SQUARE
(47) PUBLIC GARDENS & CHILDREN'S
PLAYGROUND
(48) FRUIT & VEGETABLE MARKET
(49) AKROPOLIS-PANORAMIC VIEWS
(50) PARKING AREA
(51) STADIUM
(52) ATHLETIC FIELDS
(53) FIRE CLUB (CYDIVE)
(54) MINING CLUB
(55) MUNICIPAL BATHS
(56) C.T.O. PUBLIC BEACH
(57) SODAP WINERY
(P) PETROL STATION
(S) SCHOOL
(B) BANK
PO) POST OFFICE

ACCOMMODATION ESTABLISHMENTS
(57) ANNABELLE HOTEL
(58) PAPHOS BEACH HOTEL
(59) CYPRIA MARIS HOTEL
(60) ALOE HOTEL
(61) DIONYSOS HOTEL
(62) KISSOS HOTEL
(63) VERONICA HOTEL
(64) APOLLO HOTEL
(65) AXIOTHEA HOTEL
(66) KINGS HOTEL
(67) NEW OLYMPUS HOTEL
(68) THEOPHANO HOTEL
(69) AGAPINOR HOTEL
(70) PYRAMOS HOTEL
(71) KINYRAS HOTEL
(72) PAPHOS PALACE HOTEL

(75) DAPHNE APARTMENTS
(76) DEMETRA APARTMENTS
(77) RANIA BEACH APARTMENT
(78) SOFIANA APARTMENTS
(79) MYROFORI APARTMENTS
(80) THESEAS APARTMENTS
(81) LOUKAS NEOKLEOUS APARTS
(82) PAPHOS GARDENS
(83) BASILICA GARDENS
(84) PORTO GARDENS
(85) KANIKA COMPLEX
(86) LORDOS HOTEL COMPLEX
expected by 1989

Part Two:
KATO PAPHOS (Nea Paphos — Harbour)

TOURING KATO PAPHOS

General view of Harbour

Nea Paphos, well-known to the natives as Kato Paphos, is situated about two miles south of Paphos town (Ktima). It was established as a major town with fortifications and was also an important port during the 4th Century BC. This was due to the fact that King Nicocles of Palea Paphos moved the political and commercial activities to the new town. However, the port was active before the 4th Century BC, since the pilgrims to the Holy Temple of Aphrodite, seven miles to the east at Paleapaphos, disembarked here. It is believed that the town was founded in 1180 BC by Agapenor. The port and surrounding area flourished during the Hellenistic, Ptolemaic and Roman periods. The whole area is scattered with remains of the past, an archaeological paradise for any visitor.

It is also worth mentioning here that it is believed that the ancient harbour during the Hellenistic and Roman times covered the area from the existing harbour to the area of Moulia Rocks to the South East. British underwater Army divers surveyed the area in 1959 and discovered traces of the old harbour and walls of the now submerged under deep water, breakwater walls.

Nea Paphos, the tourist part of the two towns, has tasteful hotels and holiday apartments, flats and tourist shops, banks, tavernas, restaurants and cafes and provides entertainment to satisfy every visitor.

View of the Castle from the pier

Pleasure and Fishing boats in the Harbour.

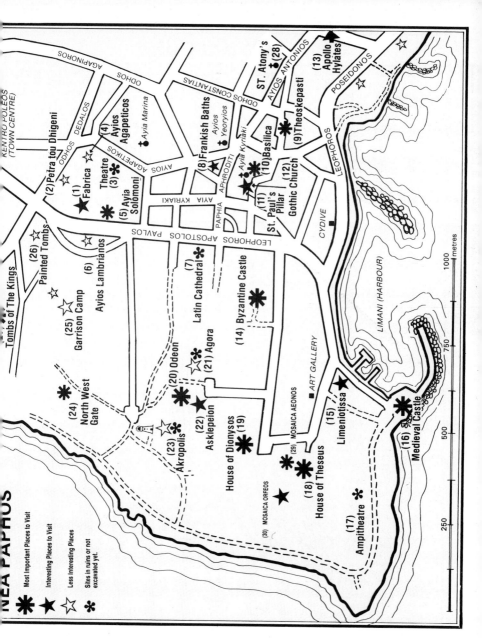

NEA PAPHOS (map title, vertical)

Legend:

✳ Most Important Places to Visit

★ Interesting Places to Visit

☆ Less Interesting Places

✱ Sites in ruins or not excavated yet.

Map labels:
- KENTRO POLEOS (TOWN CENTRE)
- ODHOS AGAPINOROS
- ODHOS DEDALOS
- (2) Petra tou Dhigeni ☆
- (1) Fabrica ★
- Theatre ☆
- (3) ✳
- (4) Ayios Agapeticos ★
- Ayia Marina
- ODHOS AGAPETIKOS
- ODHOS AYIAS KYRIAKI
- (5) Ayia Solomoni ✳
- Frankish Baths ★ (8)
- Ayios Yeoryios
- Ayia Kyriaki
- ODHOS CONSTANTIAS
- ST. Atony's (28) ♦ AYIOS ANTONIOS
- (13) Apollo Hylates ★
- POSEIDONOS
- Basilica ★ (10)
- (9) Theoskepasti ✳
- Ayia Aphroditi
- LEOPHOROS APOSTOLOS PAVLOS
- St. Paul's Pillar (11)
- (12) Gothic Church
- LEOPHOROS PAPHIA
- CYDIVE
- LEOPHOROS POSEIDONOS
- (26) Painted Tombs ☆
- (25) Garrison Camp ☆
- (6) Ayios Lambrianos
- (7) Latin Cathedral ✱
- Byzantine Castle ✳ (14)
- Tombs of The Kings
- (24) North West Gate ✳
- (20) Odeon ☆
- (21) Agora ☆
- ART GALLERY ■
- LIMANI (HARBOUR)
- (23) Akropolis ☆ ✱
- (22) Asklepeion ★
- (19) House of Dionysos ✳
- MOSAICA AEONOS (29)
- (15) Limeniotissa ★
- (16) Medieval Castle ✳
- (18) House of Theseus ★
- MOSAICA ORFEOS (30)
- (17) Ampitheatre ✱
- metres scale: 250, 500, 750, 1000

NEA PAPHOS – PLACES OF INTEREST

Many of the places described in the following pages are within walking distance from most hotels and apartments and some are connected with a bus service. Alternatively, a taxi will take you to the place or places of your choice and collect you afterwards. Excavations continue all the time

Silver Ptolemaic coin from the Paphos mint.
(Courtesy Cyprus Museum)

17

NEA PAPHOS

The last Cinyraid King of Paleapaphos moved his headquarters here in c. 320 BC and established a new tow
and a larger harbour which later served the Ptolemies, the Romans, the Crusaders and the Latins. During th
Ptolemaic and Roman periods it was the capital of Cyprus and it saw great prosperity and served both fleet
In all, it enjoyed prosperity and power for about 500 years.
During the Byzantine period it suffered from extensive Arab raids and after the raids of Abu-l'-Awar in 65
monuments and churches were destroyed. A garrison of about 12,000 men stayed here up to the 680's.
It was revived during the medieval Lusignan conquest of Cyprus between 12-16th centuries and the harbou
played an important role in the communications and the supplies of ships for the crusaders and the Genoe
fleet. Thus a commercial and military presence was established and buildings, churches and the Lat
Cathedral were amongst the best in Cyprus; sadly however nothing remains. Systematic excavations starte
in 1951 and continued ever since have unearthed very interesting ruins, however many more are still covere
and the area is protected from buildings.
Below we list the most important places which you can visit, if you stay in a hotel, apartment within the town,
early morning or late afternoon walk will take you to most of the places.

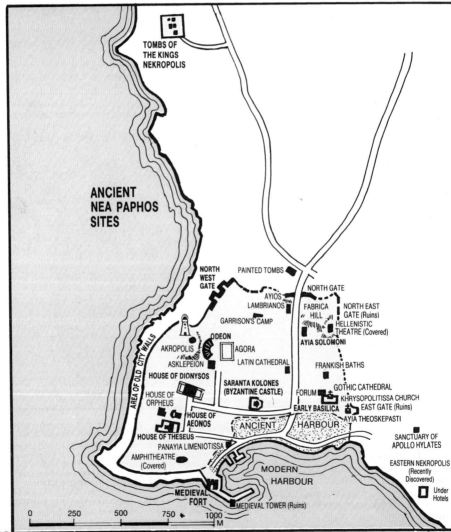

(1) FABRICA HILL

This hill lies at the entrance to Kato Paphos village, along the main road from the town of Paphos (Ktima), and forms the north east limits of the ancient city walls. These rocks are interesting due to several underground rock-cut caves and chambers. Some of the caves have vaulted roofs and plastered walls, which may have been painted. Some are large. They date back to the Hellenistic period, as far as the 3rd Century BC. No clear evidence exists for the purpose of the chambers. The public is free to visit them at any time.

(2) PETRA TOU DHIGENI
(Dhigenis Rock)

This rock (Petra tou. Dhigeni), which lies on another smaller rock in a most peculiar way, is situated to the north of Fabrica Hill and has a very interesting legend attached to it. There was once a medieval Greek hero called Dhigenis who had tremendous physical power.

During his stay in Cyprus he visited the Queen of Paphos, Rhigena, and fell in love with her beauty. The town of Paphos was suffering from a shortage of water and the Queen asked Dhigenis to bring water from the mountain and, if he succeeded, she would marry him. After much hard work Dhigenis managed to succeed with the task, only to discover that Queen Rhigena had changed her mind. In his anger he ran up the hill of Moutallos over-looking the kingdom of Paphos and, with his powerful little finger, he threw the rock at the Queen. He failed to hit her and she, in turn, threw her distaff at him, but missed her target. Eventually they got together and lived as a couple near the cave of Ayios Agapetikos.

(3) THE THEATRE

The Theatre lies to the south east of Fabrica Hill and is still covered with earth. Plans are made for future excavation and restoration. The Theatre was built in a commanding position, with a good view of the sea and town. According to a Hellenistic inscription found in the area the date of the Theatre is thought to be the 3rd Century BC.

(4) THE HERMITAGE OF AYIOS AGAPETIKOS

This interesting cave, hewn out of rock above ground, lies on the eastern slopes of Fabrica Hill and is one of the earliest Christian monuments in Paphos. Apart from being a religious area it is also dedicated to the Protector of Lovers (Ayios Agapetikos). Even today lovers go to the cave to light a candle and pray.

(5) AYIA SOLOMONI CATACOMB

This well known catacomb, unique of its type in Cyprus, lies along the main road to Kato, Paphos, south of Fabrica Hill and close to the Apollo Hotel. Steps lead down from an open courtyard to underground caves carved deep into the earth. The origin of the catacomb goes back to the Hellenistic period and was also used at later dates. Originally, it is believed it was used as a burial ground but in later times as a refuge for people, mainly Christians, during the Roman persecutions. It was at that time that it was dedicated to Ayia Solomoni and it became a church and place of worship. The legend explains that Solomoni, a devoted Christian mother pursued by the Romans, found refuge with her sons in a catacomb. The Romans when they discovered her hiding place, sealed off the caves and she was buried there with her sons. There is another version though which says that Solomoni (Hannah) was Jewish and living in Palestine. Her seven children were tortured to death in Palestine by the Romans, around 168 AD. The local Jews established this as her synagogue which was later abandoned and used by the Christians for protection. As a chapel and place of worship the chambers were decorated with impressive wall paintings during the 12th Century AD, but most of these have been damaged by the weather. Names of Crusader soldiers were scratched on both the paintings and the walls, thus inflicting more damage. Futher steps lead down to a Holy Well. The catacomb is open to both worshippers and the general public.

6) AYIOS LAMBRIANOS

This catacomb lies on the other side of the road from Ayia Solomoni, and opposite the Apollo Hotel. There is an open courtyard, surrounded by chambers and graves, similar to other tombs in the area.

(7) THE LATIN CATHEDRAL (GALATARIOTISSA)

Another impressive church, which was unfortunately destroyed. It was built in the Gothic style around the 14th Century and later restored by Francesco Contarini, the Last Latin Bishop of Paphos, who was removed after the Turkish occupation. Nothing now remains of this Cathedral, except one thick column.

(8) THE FRANKISH BATHS

This small, medieval building with a domed roof is situated close to the Sofi-Anna apartments and was built during the Lusignan period (1191-1489 AD). It served as public baths, accommodating up to 100 people daily.

General view of the Frankish Bath.

(9) PANAYIA THEOSKEPASTI

Very close to Ayia Kyriaki stands the impressive church of Panayia Theoskepasti (All Holy Virgin Mary). It is built on a rock and during the Arab raids it is said that a miraculous cloud covered the church, thus rendering it invisible to the enemy. It is also believed to be the church of the "Shrouded Madonna". The exsisting church was built in 1922, after the original one was destroyed. The church is open to the public and visitors to it will enjoy the beautiful icons and interior decorations.

(10) EARLY CHRISTIAN BASILICA CHURCH

The church which now stands on this site and is of architectural interest is called Ayia Kyriaki, built around the 13th Century in typical Byzantine style: it is open to the public. The church was built on the remains of an earlier Basilica built in the 4th Century AD was one of the largest in Cyprus and many remains, including floors and huge granite columns can be seen at the side of the existing church. Some of the floors show paving in interesting geometric mosaics. Futher excavations continue and the area is not open to the public; however, the remains can be seen clearly from the road.

(11) ST. PAULS PILLAR

The pillar, which is believed to be that of St. Paul, can be seen to the west of Ayia Kyriaki Church. This pillar has a special significance since it was alleged that St. Paul, during his visit to Paphos in 45 AD to preach Christianity, was bound to it as punishment and given 39 lashes — "Saranta para mia" — as the Greeks say to this day. Afterwards, in his anger, St. Paul punished the local Jewish religious leader, Elymas — who masterminded the punishment — by blinding him.

The Roman Governor, Sergius-Paulus, was then converted to Christianity, thus becoming the first important Roman in the whole Empire to embrace the new religion. The surrounding remains are thought to be those of the Roman Forum.

(12) GOTHIC CHURCH

The remains of the Gothic Church are to the south east of St Paul's Pillar and close to the Christian Basilica on the other side of the road. This church, built in Latin style around 1300 AD, was probably used by the Franciscan Convent of Paphos. Some Renaissance-style statues found here date back to the 15th Century. When the Turks occupied Cyprus the church was turned into a Mosque but it collapsed towards the end of the 16th Century. Floor remains and some walls can be seen.

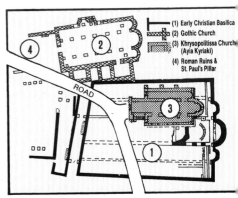

(1) Early Christian Basilica
(2) Gothic Church
(3) Khrysopolitissa Church (Ayia Kyriaki)
(4) Roman Ruins & St. Paul's Pillar

Plan of the Early Christian Basilica and Gothic Cathedral.

A painting showing **St. Paul** (left) blinding **Elymas** (right) while the Roman governor **Sergius Paulus** (centre) watches with astonishment and then became converted to Christianity.
This most important early Christian event gave strength and expansion to Christianity in Paphos and Cyprus.

General view of the Byzantine castle with views of the various rooms

Left: St Pauls Pillar where it is believed he was tied and lashed. Above: Theoskepasti Church as seen from the rear, built on rock, which was part of Eastern city fortifications.

Early Christian Basilica and the Church of Ayia Kyriaki

The Odeon, where plays and cultural events take place at times.

Left, Top: Ayios Agapetikos Hermitage, Bottom: The Dhigenis Rock. Above: The entrance to Ayia Solomoni Catacombs.

21

(13) SANCTURY OF APOLLO HYLATES

These rock-cut underground chambers which lie south east of the East Gate and north of Paphos Beach Hotel, are the sanctuary of Apollo Hylates. Inscriptions are to be seen in Cypro-Syllabic script cut above the entrance, which explain that the cave is dedicated to Apollo Hylates by the High Priest Dajaphas the Ajaros. The caves date back to the 4th Century BC. For many years the sanctuary, which stands amongst pine and cypress trees, was a sacred spot. The sanctuary is situated on private property but when the area was visited by the author, the gate was open and no one was around. Should you have any problem in getting to the sanctuary, please contact the museum for advice.

(14) BYZANTINE CASTLE

Overlooking the harbour stands the castle which, it is believed, dates back to the 7th Century AD and built in order to protect the port and town against the Arab raids. The locals also call it "Saranta Kolones" (forty columns), because of the number of broken granite columns found lying around.

Recent excavations have revealed more of the castle, the walls, the various quarters and rooms, courtyards and underground chambers. It is open to he public at all times and the visitor is requested to take great care to avoid any damage. When Richard The Lion Heart occupied Cyprus in 1191 AD the castle surrendered to him, but eventually it was destroyed by an earthquake in 1222 AD.

The castle had eight towers of different shapes defending the thick outer walls. Part of the castle has been restored.

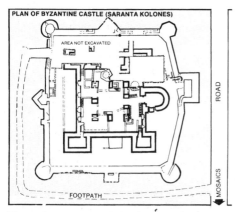

Plan o the Byzantine Castle of Saranta Kolones.

(15) PANAYIA LIMENIOTISSA

The remains of this early Christian Basilica lie very close to the harbour and just behind the restaurants. It dates back to the 5th century AD and is dedicated to Panayia Limeniotissa (Our Lady of The Port). Floor mosaics and wall foundations can be seen from the road.

Remains of the Panayia Limeniotissa Basilica which was demolished by the Arabs, restored in later times and then destroyed.

(16) THE MEDIEVAL CASTLE

Commanding a view of the southern part of the harbour is the Medieval Castle, which is visible from all directions. It was built by the Lusignans in the 13th Century AD to replace the destroyed Byzantine Castle. It was partially destroyed by the defending Venetians in 1570 AD, but the Turkish victors restored and fortified it soon afterwards.

The extension, which is further along the breakwater, is in ruins since it was never restored. Above the entrance to the Castle is an Arabic saying written in 1592 — "By the Goodness of God, the Honourable Ahmet Pasha — Hafouz of the Truthful Koran — erected the Castle of Paphos and left a Good Religious Work. This very strong castle. May God Benefit his establisher said. . . ." (Atel is the name of the poet who wrote the inscription.) KALAI BAFTIR BIR HISNI HASIN — translated it means — The Castle of Paphos is a very Strong Castle.

The Castle is now restored and open to the public. From the top one can enjoy a wonderful view of the harbour and surrounding area.

(17) AMPHITHEATRE

Behind the Castle and the Customs House used to lie the Amphitheatre. All that is visible now is the oval-shaped depression in the ground. Some foundations were discovered but practically everything surviving is still buried.

Above: The Byzantine Castle of Saranta Kolones — *Below:* Another view of the Medieval Castle which dominates the harbour and is open to the public daily — An old 19th century engraving.

THE MOSAIC HOUSES

These are probably the most interesting places to visit in Paphos. Current excavations are being concentrated on the two houses — the house of Theseus and the house of Dionysos. They are both situated close to one another between the harbour, the lighthouse (Acropolis) and the Meteorological Station. As the latest mosaics show the whole area it is certain that it contains many more mosaic floors waiting to be discovered in the near future.

(19) THE HOUSE OF DIONYSOS

It is believed that this was once a private house (Roman villa) and dates back to the second half of the 2nd Century AD. It was accidentally discovered in 1962 by a farmer ploughing his fields. This house is of enormous importance since most of the floors have mosaic scenes depicting characters from Greek mythology, and their artistic value places them amongst the finest in the world. This house is so beautiful that it is visited by art lovers from all over the world. The United States AID Mission helped with finance to erect the protective shelter.

Some of the mosaic scenes include the following:

The Triumph of Dionysos

Dionysos, God of Wine and Happiness, sits crowned with vine leaves in a chariot drawn by two wild beasts. Following behind is a satyr with an amphora full of wine, Pan, a young negro and two maenads. More figures can be seen in front of the chariot and the last figure is that of a young man sounding a trumpet:— "The Triumph of Dionysos".

Above: Silver Ptolemaic coins as found at the House of Dionysos. Below:

Dionysos, Akme and Ikarios

Here the God is seated on a stool offering grapes to Nymph Akme, who is drinking from a bowl (wine, of course!). Next to her Ikarios is leading an ox-driven cart loaded with flasks full of wine. Behind the cart are two drunken men — "The First Wine Drinkers" — as the inscription above them explains. According to legend Dionysos visited the Palace of the King of Athens, Ikarios, where he taught him the art of making wine.

The Triumph of Dionysos, scene from the house of Dionysos (courtesy, the Director of Antiquities)

While the King was taking the wine to the Athenians he met with two shepherds, to whom he offered a drink. They were not used to wine and, once they became drunk they thought the King was trying to poison them and they killed him.

Pyramus and Thisbe

This mosaic shows Thisbe standing frightened staring at a panther (wild beast) that is running away, carrying a cloth in its mouth. Pyramus, crowned with reeds, lays dying on the ground holding a cornucopia. Here the legends says that Pyramus and Thisbe were two lovers who were forbidden by their parents to marry. One day Thisbe, on her way to their meeting place, was attacked by a wild beast. She was injured but managed to escape. Unfortunately she left behind a blood-stained veil. When Pyramus arrived at the scene he found the veil and, believing that his love had been killed, he took his own life. Later Thisbe returned and found Pyramus lying dead. In her grief she also killed herself.

Other interesting scenes include: The Four Seasons — Narcissus — Poseidon and Anymone — Apollo, Daphne and Penios — Hippolytus and Phaedra — Hunting Scenes.

Please note: By the entrance, there are WC facilities.

A very comprehensive and detailed description of the House of Dionysos and the various mosaic scenes has been written by Professor G.S. Eliades, owner of the Ethnographic Museum at 1 Exo Vrisis Street, Paphos.

Above top: Mosaic floor showing Ganymede taken away by Zeus disguised as an eagle.
Above: Part of a mosaic floor showing Phaedra and Hippolytus. *(Courtesy Cyprus Museum)*

Mosaic scene of Dionysos, Akme & Ikarios and the first Wine Drinkers *(Courtesy Director of Antiquities)*

Mosaic scene of Peneus, Apollo & Daphne. Apollo was madly in love with Daphne's beauty. However, Daphne was not interested and to avoid Apollo, she asked help from Zeus who transformed her into a laurel flower. The transformation started taking place as seen on her feet. Peneus to the left (Daphne's father) is watching.

Mosaic scene of the Love Tragedy of Pyramos and Thisbe as shown in this outstanding example of mosaic art. Story description on page 25.

(18) THE HOUSE OF THESEUS

This site gets its name from the well-preserved floor mosaic of the mythological hero Theseus slaying the Minotaur. All the rooms were paved with mosaics, although most have now been destroyed. Among other mosaic scenes to be found in the house is that of the Birth of Achilles with Ambrosia, Anatrophe, the baby Achilles, his mother Thetis and father Peleus seated on the throne and followed by the Three Fates — Clotho, Lachesis and Atropos. The mosaic depicting Theseus slaying the Minotaur shows Theseus in the centre ready to kill the Minotaur which lies at his feet. Busts of Ariadne and Crete can also be seen. It dates back to around the 2nd Century AD. Excavations continue.

Theseus slaying the Minotaur, scene from the house of Theseus (courtesy, Director of Antiquities).

Mosaic Representing the bath of Achilles from the House of Theseus.

HOUSE OF AION (AEON). These new finds of mosaics just to the north entrance to the House of Theseus are of excellent artistic presentation and show the birth and protection of baby DIONYSOS, LEDA and KYKNOS and AEON as the Judge of a beauty contest in the middle of the mosaic and to his left is CASSIOPEIA the winner and to the right the NYMPHS of the sea the loosers.

The mosaics are covered for protection and open to the public who may obtain entrance tickets at the main entrance of the House of Dionysos. The same ticket covers both houses.

HOUSE OF ORPHEUS. This house is situated close to the House of Theseus (to the west). It was accidently discovered during World War II but its systematic excavation started only in 1982. It is only partly excavated but excellent mosaics have already come to light. These include an **Amazon, Hercules and the Lion** and an excellent **Orpheus** charming the wild Beasts with his music. The name of the house was given from the scene of this Mosaic as *"The House of Orpheus"*.

The mosaics will be opened to visitors shortly.

Above and right: Two scenes of the beautiful mosaics from the **House of AEON.** These mosaics are of excellent artistic presentation and date to the same periods as the other Mosaics of Dionysos and Theseus.

With the kind permission of Dr. W.A. Daszewski, Polish Archaeological Mission.

House of Orpheus: Mosaic showing Orpheus playing music and charming the wild beasts. With the kind permission of Dr. D. Michaelides.

(20) THE ODEON

Excavated and now restored, the Odeon is one of the most impressive monuments of Paphos. In the summer local theatre clubs perform ancient Greek plays and it is worth enquiring at your hotel for the dates. The first play was performed on 29th June 1975 by local students. The play MEDEA by Eurepides was directed by C. Kakoyiannis. The Odeon was built entirely of stone with a semi-circular orchestra around the 2nd Century AD. Originally it had 25 tiers and seated 3000 people. It can now accommodate up to 1200 people.

(21) THE AGORA

Dated at the same period as the Odeon the Agora stands in front of the Theatre. It has been partially excavated and only foundations can be seen, with some granite columns lying on the ground. The Agora was used mainly for shopping and gatherings.

(22) THE ASKLEPEION

Next to the Odeon is the Asklepeion building where more can be seen than in the Agora. It consists of three parts of corridors, large rooms and some unspoilt chambers. Excavations are continuing on this site. The Asklepeion, the only one found in Cyprus, was dedicated to the God of Medicine and Healing — ASKLEPEIOS. As a God he could heal practically anything and he was helped by special powers such as from snakes and his four daughters: HYGIA (Health); IASSO (Therapy); EGLI (The Bright One) and PANAYIA (All Cure).

The Asklepeion was the Temple and the place where the God was worshipped. It was also the place for treatment and used as a school for teaching. Doctors performed cures after following a strict programme of internal and external cleansing.

(23) THE ACROPOLIS (LIGHTHOUSE)

There can be no ancient city without the Acropolis (the highest rock spot where a temple always stood) and Paphos is no exception. Unfortunately no temple exists now but some remains of the Hellenistic and Roman periods have recently been found. On the rock now stands a lighthouse and some houses, which make an interesting complex. Rock-cut steps can be seen on the side of the Odeon leading down from the Acropolis to the Theatre.

(24) THE CITY WALL

The City Wall which surrounded the town as shown on the map has been more or less destroyed. Some traces can be seen around Fabrica Hill, but most important are those behind the lighthouse (Acropolis). At this point the wall followed the edge of the rocky cliffs, which protected it from the sea. The North West gate which lies here was cut from the rock and one can see the remains of a bridge by this gate. Excavations are under way which may throw more light on the old defences of the town.

(25) GARRISON'S CAMP

More complex underground rock-cut caves can be seen near Ayios Lambrianos, most of them still to be excavated. They resemble the Apollo Sanctuary but there is no evidence to justify this identification positively. The date of origin is believed to be the 4th Century BC and it is widely held that this area was used as a main base for various armies as a camp, including the Egyptian Ptolemaic troops and the Romans.

(26) PAINTED TOMBS

These tombs were discovered recently whilst some construction was under way. They are to remain open for the public to view. They are close to the Garrison Camp rocks. The walls and ceilings of both tombs were painted with flora and geometric patterns. The two tombs date back to the Hellenistic period and it is believed that they were also used at later dates.

(28) ST. ANTHONY'S CHURCH

This small church is in St. Anthony Street and is leased out by the Bishopric of Paphos to the Anglican Church for regular services by the British community of Paphos.

Above: The fenced Garrison's camp. There are a couple in the area and many others still covered. *Below:* Part of the recently excavated North West city walls.

The Churches of Kato Paphos: *Above:* The church of Ayia Kyriaki (Khrysopolitissa Church) — see Early Christian Basilica page 20. *Below:* The church of Panayia Theoskepasti, page 20.

The remains of the Agora and the now restored ODEON. The lighthouse in the background stands on the Acropolis.

The two castles of Paphos; Above: The Medieval Castle. Below: The Byzantine Castle.

Modern Kato Paphos: The modern town of Kato Paphos, has been expanding very rapidly since the early 80's and although it offers most modern amenities for the tourists, it has unfortunately resulted in covering the eastern part of the ancient city and the eastern Nekropolis with Hotels and other buildings. However many of the tombs within Annabelle and Kanika hotels and the surrounding area have been preserved and visitors can visit them. The new town offers a variety of shops, souvenir shops, eating places, pubs, entertainment, discos, and it is an ideal place for visitors to explore.

Above: Sunsets in Paphos are beautiful and idylic. This scene is as seen from the Gardens of Paphos Beach Hotel. *Below:* Part of Poseidonos Avenue with cafes, restaurants and souvenir shops.

(27) TOMBS OF THE KINGS

These rock-cut tombs, unique of their type in Cyprus, are situated north west of the town of Kato Paphos and form an impressive Necropolis with caves, chambers, fascinating rock formations and tombs. Most of the area is still covered and is to be excavated.

The tombs, with heavy Doric-style columns and chambers cut in the rock below ground level, were used as a burial ground in the Hellenistic period (3rd Century BC) and later by the Romans. During the Christian persecutions by the Romans some tombs were used as a refuge.

They were further used during Medieval times and some changes were made. Severe looting occured at various times which caused the destruction of many important items. The site was also used as a quarry, thus inflicting more damage to the tombs. Excavations were carried out between 1937 and 1951 but, due to the lack of professional and scholarly supervision, practically all the evidence discovered was then lost. Very careful and systematic excavations are being carried out at present and new types of tombs have been discovered. However, a tour of the Necropolis is a must for every visitor, archaeology lover or not, since it combines a unique beauty with a natural and fascinating setting. Although the tombs are called Tombs of The Kings, no evidence has yet been found that they were used for the burial of Royalty.

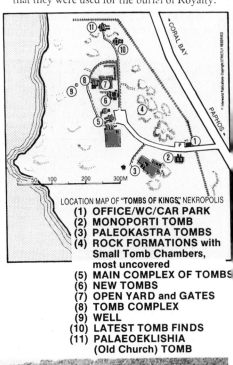

LOCATION MAP OF "TOMBS OF KINGS" NEKROPOLIS

(1) OFFICE/WC/CAR PARK
(2) MONOPORTI TOMB
(3) PALEOKASTRA TOMBS
(4) ROCK FORMATIONS with Small Tomb Chambers, most uncovered
(5) MAIN COMPLEX OF TOMBS
(6) NEW TOMBS
(7) OPEN YARD and GATES
(8) TOMB COMPLEX
(9) WELL
(10) LATEST TOMB FINDS
(11) PALAEOEKLISHIA (Old Church) TOMB

Another tomb from the "Tombs of the King's area. Each tomb has its own characteristic.

Various types of Tombs from the Valley of the
TOMBS OF KINGS — one of the most popular
archaeological sites of Cyprus.

CHAPTER 3

EXPLORING THE COUNTRYSIDE

With this Guide you can explore the parts of Paphos you wish to see and by the route, the way you prefer. If you don't have a car, you can arrange to hire a taxi for a day. The taxi driver will either take you and leave you at your destination and return to pick you up in the evening, or he will drive you around.

Even if you are staying in other parts of Cyprus such as Limassol, visiting some places in Paphos is a must, and please remember, it takes only about an hour to drive from Limassol to Paphos town. Some tourist companies and tourist agencies offer tours to the most popular places. You can contact them for information.

The beautiful Paphos district offers a bit for everybody, the beaches of Coral Bay or Chrysochou Bay or Aphrodites Baths, the mountains, the villages, the monasteries . . .

Hoggarth wrote the following in his book DEVIA CYPRIA in 1887-88 when he visited Paphos and explored the countryside.

"Nature has defined it so clearly that we can hardly mistake the boundaries in spite of written authority. On the north and west lies the sea. Upon the east, the mass of Troodos continued in the rugged forest to Pomos Point, interposed a huge barrier between the west and the east of the island, which even under Evagoras, the Kingdom of Salamis appears not to have passed. At the northern end of this barrier, the kingdom of Paphos marched with that of Soloi. Lastly, upon the south, the tremendous cleft, cut by the Kostitheos river (a name not appearing in todays maps) up to mount Troodos, bounds the Kingdom of Curium . . . ."

PLEASE REMEMBER

If you drive, be careful, make sure that you have plenty of fuel (petrol stations are closed on Saturday afternoons, Sundays and holidays). Check the tyres, take plenty of water and a torch for the night. Also take drinking water as the heat makes you thirsty. In the KAFENION of the village (the pub of Cyprus), which you cannot miss as it is always situated in the square, you will find refreshments. For eating if you are away from the main tourist areas it is advisable to take sandwiches etc., as you may not be able to find a place to have a cooked meal.

If you explore the countryside on foot, please take high boots with you for there is a rare chance you may disturb a snake, some are harmless but some are poisonous. Carry basic medical supplies and provisions for eating and drinking and if you plan to spend the night out, a sleeping bag.

Whether you are in the country or by the beach, do not expose your skin and head too much to the sun, especially during the first few days of your stay. Sun burns are very unpleasant and the sun is very strong.

VISITING OTHER PARTS OF CYPRUS

Although it is far to travel to **Ayia Napa**, you can go to **NICOSIA** in just over 2 hours and if you leave early in the morning you can be in the capital by 8 or 9am giving you plenty of time for a stroll around the shops or a visit to the **Cyprus Museum**, then return by late afternoon. Or you can explore the **TROODOS** mountains and visit the best and largest monastery of Cyprus (**Kykko Monastery**) although avoid such a journey around 14-16 August when all the locals drive there for a festival. You can visit the famous **TEMPLE OF APOLLO HYLATES** and the ancient city of **CURIUM** with its beautiful theatre. Further away towards Limassol is **KOLOSSI CASTLE** with its fascinating medieval architecture. And **Limassol** town is only just over an hours drive from Paphos.

ROUTE A ON THE FOOTSTEPS OF APHRODITE

Roman Coin representing the Temple of Aphrodite *(Courtesy Cyprus Museum)*

The route from Paphos to Petra tou Romiou (the famous birthplace of Aphrodite) demands careful driving and observation of the road signs, since this is the very busy main road between Paphos and Limassol. Always remember to take extra care. However, it is a very pleasant trip, passing through green fields of banana, citrus trees, vines and peanuts — the only place in Cyprus where they are grown. The airport of Paphos, which is now fully operational, is on the south of the road close to the sea, near Akhelia. The journey to Petra tou Romiou is 16 miles, but various stops should be made to explore important places of interest.

YEROSKIPOS

This village is very close to the main town of Paphos now almost joined together. The worship of Aphrodite brought great importance to this small place. Here were her Holy Gardens (Yieros Kipos) where pilgrims, after disembarking at the port of Paphos, stopped to relax before continuing their journey to the Holy Temple of Paleapaphos. The village square, with cafes and souvenir shops, is always busy with people. Strolling along to the south of the square you will reach **Ayia Paraskevi Church.** This church was built in the 11th Century AD and has five domes. The interior is also very interesting with some fine wall paintings depicting scenes such as The Resurrection of Lazarus, The Entrance into Jerusalem, The Last Supper and many others. There are also some beautiful icons for the visitor to see.

Another place that one should not miss is the **Folk Art Museum** which is open daily. Between 1799 and 1864 this house was the British Consulate for the area. It is called the Haji Smith House. A Greek immigrant from the Greek island of Kephalonia, Andreas Zamboulaki, was appointed by Sir Sidney Smith, after his victory over Napoleon's army in Egypt. The appointment took place in 1799 and Adreas Zamboulaki, now as a British Consular Agent, had the job of providing the British fleet with fresh supplies and provisions when they visited Paphos. The house has interesting architectural points and is now well preserved as a Folk Art Museum. There are various items on display such as costumes, tools, wood carvings, embroidery, household items and so on.

KOLONI

This is a small village. In the past however, its soil produced earth of different colours "Terra d'umbra" which was ideal for pottery. It was

37

Above: The church of Ayia Paraskevi situated to the south of the Square at Yeroskipos Village.
Below: Woven bed sheet with cross-stitched patterns from Yeroskipos Folk Art Museum.
(Courtesy Cyprus Museum)

THE YEROSKIPOS DELIGHTS

No visitor to Yeroskipos will miss the numerous stalls on both sides of the road selling this traditional local product of "LOUKOUMIA" – Turkish Delights. The original industry was established in 1895 but the man who produuced such excellent ingredients took his secret to the grave. There are now different brands with their own distinctive taste. Ideal purchase for your home or as a gift to friends.

also at one time important for the discovery of the famous PAPHOS DIAMONDS in the nearby hills. In fact, they were not Diamonds and had no great value as they were only rock crystals of superior quality, but in those days, the Turkish authorities believed that real diamonds had been discovered and sealed off the area and posted guards to protect their new "wealth".

ANATOLIKON MONASTERY

This building, once functioning as a monastery, is now a farmhouse and acts as a centre for the surrounding farms. The medieval church of *Ayios Charalambos* is most intriguing and worth a visit.

AKHELIA

An important agricultural centre, situated by the side of the river Ezousas south of the main road. It is widely believed that the area was inhabited by ancient Greeks and Romans and during medieval times it became a major sugar producing centre and also a Commandery under the Knights Hospitallers. Later it was owned by the Venetian firm of Martoni (1450 A.D.). Under the Turks it continued as an agricultural centre called *"Akhelia Chiftlik"*. Now it is a very important agricultural station.

There are two interesting churches. *Ayios Theodosios* is pretty and of a unique Byzantine style (only four of this design exist in Cyprus). The altar contains some Roman marble. *Ayios Yeoryios* is a medieval church. There were some remarkable woodcarvings and other objects which were removed and sold in auctions in London around 1900. Only a few icons now exist.

TIMI (see under route B3)

The Paphos International Airport

Nicely situated, close to the sea and south of Akhelia and Timi, this new ultra-modern airport also possesses a long runway suitable for the biggest jets. It started official direct flights to the U.K., Greece and other places for tourist traffic in April 1984. It is also used for transporting agricultural products.

MANDRIA

An agricultural centre south of the main road with some 400 inhabitants. There is a church that is worth a visit with a strange marble capital and a female head above the west door. To the south east of the village there is a small chapel, *Ayia Arkona*, built on top of an ancient site.

Further south, near the sea there are further remains of old ruins, some possibly submerged under water. Please note that to the north east of this area is Paleapaphos and it is believed that a small harbour was in operation from cape Zephyros and along the eastern coast.

There is an old quarry in the area and also some strange **MONOLITHS**, the largest of which is about 10 feet high above ground and pierced with holes. Similar types of stones are to be found in some other parts of Paphos and Cyprus. Although one simple theory is that they were used as oil mills, they are still surrounded with mystery.

The Church of Ayios Theodosios — Akhelia.

The Ancient Kingdom of
PALEAPAPHOS

General view of the ruins of the Temple of Aphrodite

KOUKLIA (PALEAPAPHOS)

The highlight of this particular trip is the visit to this once very famous place, Kouklia. This was the centre for the worship of Aphrodite and pilgrims came here from all over the Mediterranean. Make sure you do not miss the turning (to the left as you come from Paphos) since it is on a bend, though it is well sign-posted.

Above: The Lusignan Manor House as seen from the fields. Below: The entrance to the manor, as seen from the inside courtyard. The building houses the local museum where finds for the surrounding area are on display.

The old town was situated in a commanding position on a flat-topped hill overlooking the valley and the sea, which is about one mile to the south. The view from the top is excellent. The town of Kouklia was established by Agapenor, King of Tegea (Arcadia — Greece). There is evidence though from recently discovered tombs around the area that a settlement was established there much earlier and some form of worshipping was already in progress. The legend says that Pygmalion, one of the kings of the town, was also a good sculptor and carved many statues. Eventually he fell passionately in love with one of them, so much so that Aphrodite decided to turn the statue into a real woman and gave it life. From this relationship was born a son, Paphos, thus giving his name to the Town.

However, the most famous man of Palea-paphos was Kinyras, who is believed to have

Remains of the Temple of Aphrodite believed to be dated to around 1200 B.C.

been the major influence behind the newly-emerged Cypriot civilisation. Under his direction many new inventions were created using metals, and he also placed a lot of emphasis on music and musical instruments. As the High Priest of the Temple he introduced further mysteries into the religious festivities, most of which he brought from Egypt.

As a religious centre, for the worship of the Goddess of Love, Paleapaphos attracted a great number of famous and influential people. In the Temple there was a granite stone — a sacred cone of phallic shape (now on display in the Nicosia Museum) — which made Paleapaphos the centre of the world for the worshippers of Aphrodite.

During the festivals the cone was annointed with oil. The Priestesses of Love (the only people, apart from the High Priest, who were allowed access to the cone) would then dry it carefully with soft towels. No-one else was allowed to see the cone, which was regarded as sacred and covered with veils.

Various ceremonies took place over the year — The **Zakoria** probably the ceremony for the servants; The **Perioria** — before the main ceremonies and The **Aphrodisia.**

The Aphrodisia Festivities were an annual event and worshippers from all over the world would gather at Yeroskipos, in the Holy Gardens. From there they would follow the Holy Route towards Paleapaphos and the Temple. Many were spectators, but some were to take part in the four-day Mysteries.

During the first day sports and games were dedicated to the candidates.

On the second day they bathed in the sea to the south of the town.

The third day was spent in the Temple with prayers and offerings of fruit, flowers and grain laid before the covered cone — the symbol of Aphrodite.

The final day of the Mysteries was the initiation. The worshipper gave the Priest a coin in exchange for a lump of salt. This exchange symbolised the birth of Aphrodite from the foam of the sea. The Priest then commenced the initiation, allowed the worshipper to enter into the Mysteries of Love by offering him a cake, and saying:

"Take this cake, symbol of the Goddess of Love and picture to yourself Aphrodite. Remember that her name is very sacred. You are not worthy even to mention it . . . she inspires . . ., she feeds you, me and everyone else. . ."

Together with the Mysteries and Rites of Aphrodite, another Festival also took

Stamp showing an ancient coin of Paphos from the 1955 set

41

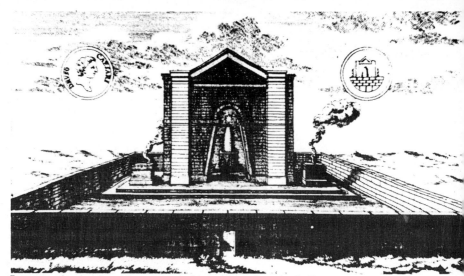

Reconstruction drawing of the sanctuary of Aphrodite as drawn by the Baroque architect J.B. Fischer Von Erhach.

place — that of the **Rites of Adonis.** Adonis, a handsome son of Kinyras and Metham, was the beloved youth of Aphrodite. But Adonis was loved not only by Aphrodite but also by Persephone, a beautiful but devilish Goddess of the underworld. Both being madly in love with Adonis, they continually quarrelled and fought each other. To put an end to this The *Court of Gods* ruled that Adonis should give one third of his life per year to Aphrodite, one third to Persephone and keep one third for himself. However, he cheated and spent his own time with Aphrodite. When Persephone found out about this she was so furious and jealous that she decided to eliminate the man she so loved. One day Adonis while out hunting in the mountains of Paphos, came across Persephone. In her fury she turned a wild boar against him and he was killed. When Aphrodite heard the bad news she became hysterical. She ran through the woods to her dying lover cutting her legs, and from the blood of her injuries and her tears lilies started to grow. . . To Adonis' memory an annual funeral procession with mourners was held on the first day of the Rites and on the following day another ceremony depicted his resurrection. There were wild celebrations afterwards for the happy event.

Paphos (Paleapaphos) remained a religious centre for 16 Centuries, although the administration was moved to Nea Paphos during the Ptolemaic period; and during Roman times, which followed. The last King who ruled over the area of Paphos was Nicocles, who moved the administration to the new city of Nea Paphos towards the end of the 4th Century. The Temple was destroyed by one of the worst earthquakes in 15 BC. The Roman Emperor Octavianus Agustus ordered its immediate restoration. The worshipping of Aphrodite and the rites were eventually put to an end by the Byzantine Emperors.

Places of interest to be seen:

The Temple: The ruins, which cover a wide area, have not yet been restored and show nothing of the impressive buildings which once stood there. The existing ruins are thought to be those of the Roman Temple which was built on the foundations of the original. A detailed description of the Temple is given in the Official Guide which one may obtain from the Museum. Some other remains were found around the Palace.

The Lusignan Manor House: This is the medieval building at the far end of the Temple which, since its restoration, is the Museum and is very interesting to visit. The Manor House was called the Château de Covocle but this was later destroyed and rebuilt by the Turks and called a Turkish Chiftlik. It housed the landlord, who administered the cultivation of the land.

The Final death blow to this so famous shrine of the Goddess Aphrodite was given by the decree of Emperor Theodosius (379-395 AD) which closed down all pagan temples and prohibited any activity related to their worshipping.

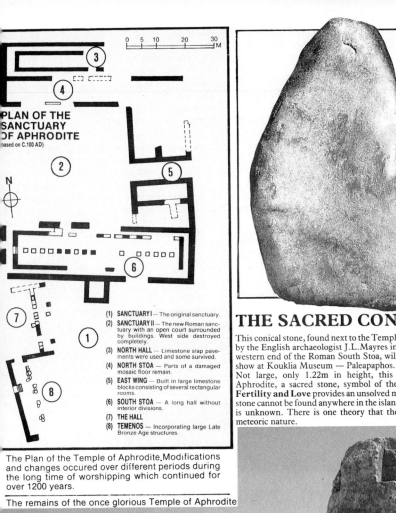

PLAN OF THE SANCTUARY OF APHRODITE
(based on C.100 AD)

N

0 5 10 20 30 M

(1) **SANCTUARY I** — The original sanctuary.

(2) **SANCTUARY II** — The new Roman sanctuary with an open court surrounded by buildings. West side destroyed completely.

(3) **NORTH HALL** — Limestone slap pavements were used and some survived.

(4) **NORTH STOA** — Parts of a damaged mosaic floor remain.

(5) **EAST WING** — Built in large limestone blocks consisting of several rectangular rooms.

(6) **SOUTH STOA** — A long hall without interior divisions.

(7) **THE HALL**

(8) **TEMENOS** — Incorporating large Late Bronze Age structures.

The Plan of the Temple of Aphrodite. Modifications and changes occured over different periods during the long time of worshipping which continued for over 1200 years.

The remains of the once glorious Temple of Aphrodite

THE SACRED CONE

This conical stone, found next to the Temple of Aphrodite by the English archaeologist J.L.Mayres in 1913 near the western end of the Roman South Stoa, will be shortly on show at Kouklia Museum — Paleapaphos.

Not large, only 1.22m in height, this Cult Idol of Aphrodite, a sacred stone, symbol of the **Goddess of Fertility and Love** provides an unsolved mystery. Such a stone cannot be found anywhere in the island and its origin is unknown. There is one theory that the stone is of a meteoric nature.

The Museum: This is housed within the Lusignan Manor House (Chiftlik). The museum, although small is interesting with items found in and around Kouklia. New rooms of the Manor which have been recently restored are to be used for more exhibits and the Grand Hall for exhibitions and seminars.

The Katholiki Church: This small, impressive church, close to the Temple ruins, has a small courtyard all round with columns and arches. The church dates from the 14th or 15th century and has interior frescoes and woodcarvings.

In the Village: In the square of the village we find the church of *Ayios Loukas*. Interesting are also some old houses.

Outside the Village: To the east and south east, along the valleys and the hills are some ancient tombs of various periods, most important being that of the *Spileon tis Regines*. To the west is a necropolis of the Bronze Age.

To the north **East Gate (site A)** on the side of Marcello Hill are to be seen the remains of the siege works and the siege ramp (see page 34) and remains of the City Walls.

Further south by Hadji Abdullah **(site B)** are remains of an important building which is said to have housed the Persian Commanders. Near by are more remains of the city walls.

To the north, some 2 miles from the road to Arkhemandrita is a cave known as **Enklistra** of an unknown hermit with his tomb. Old frescoes are visible. Near the cave are the ruins of *St. Constantine* church and a monastery.

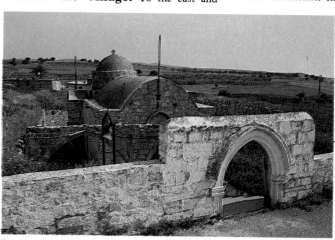

The Katholiki Church.

Bronze helmet of 5th century BC of Corinthian type, found at the siege mound near site A, now at the Cyprus Museum *(courtesy Director of Antiquities)*

LEDA & KYKNOS (SWAN)

This excellent mosaic was found at the Roman *"House of Leda"* near the Temple. It shows beautiful Leda teasing amorous Zeus who is disguised as a Swan. The mosaic is exhibited at the Cyprus Museum.

A reproduction of the mosaic has been placed on the original site which is to the west of the Temple. A visitor can take the path, west of the entrance to the Temple to reach the house due to open in early 1987.

PALEAPAPHOS — BRIEF HISTORY

The first archaeological excavations started at Kouklia by Joseph Hammer Von Purgstall in 1800 but without much success. This was followed by Luigi Palma de Cesnola between 1869-70 who inflicted much damage.

In 1888-89 the Cyprus Exploration Fund set up by the new British administration started preliminary excavations at the Temple site and also discovered various tombs nearby.

In 1950 the second British expedition started work in and around Kouklia and work by various foreign groups and the Department of Antiquities continued ever since. The latest finds are of the medieval period, the sugar cane refining installations.

Below we document a very brief chronology of the history of PALEAPAPHOS. For those who would like more detailed information which also includes Nea Paphos, we highly recommend the book by F.G. Maier & V. Karageorgis, **"Paphos-History and Archaeology"**.

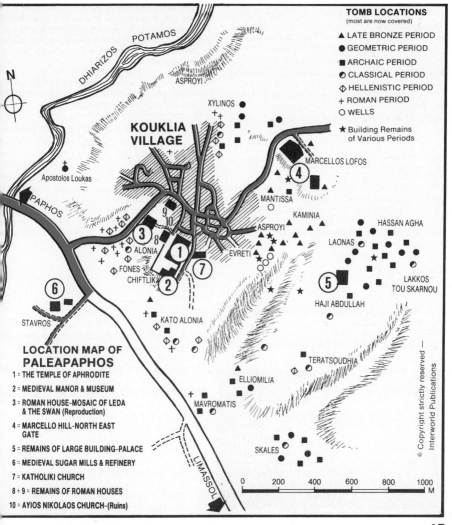

TOMB LOCATIONS
(most are now covered)

▲ LATE BRONZE PERIOD
● GEOMETRIC PERIOD
■ ARCHAIC PERIOD
◐ CLASSICAL PERIOD
◇ HELLENISTIC PERIOD
+ ROMAN PERIOD
○ WELLS
★ Building Remains of Various Periods

LOCATION MAP OF PALEAPAPHOS

1 = THE TEMPLE OF APHRODITE
2 = MEDIEVAL MANOR & MUSEUM
3 = ROMAN HOUSE-MOSAIC OF LEDA & THE SWAN (Reproduction)
4 = MARCELLO HILL-NORTH EAST GATE
5 = REMAINS OF LARGE BUILDING-PALACE
6 = MEDIEVAL SUGAR MILLS & REFINERY
7 = KATHOLIKI CHURCH
8 + 9 = REMAINS OF ROMAN HOUSES
10 = AYIOS NIKOLAOS CHURCH-(Ruins)

45

CHALCOLITHIC PERIOD c. 2800BC.

Finds at Asproyi and Evreti areas show that some habitation existed during that period.

LATE BRONZE AGE 1650-1050BC.

Cinyras was the founder King of the pre-Greek population although the exact date is unknown. Finds at various tombs to the east of the town date to various periods of this age.

The **Greek Achaeans** settled here in the 12th century and assumed their role in the city although the Cinyrad dynasty continued as Rulers and High Priests for many hundreds of years.

The first sanctuary, it was believed, was established c. 1200BC although its origins are shrouded in mystery.

The 11th century was a big turning point when the Greek settlers assumed their dominant role upon the city, mainly in culture and commerce as the Temple continued with an Eastern influence.

CYPRO-GEOMETRIC PERIOD

1050-750BC. This period is not very well documented and is regarded as the "dark ages"

ARCHAIC PERIOD 750-475BC.

A new revival. The city sees expansion. Fortifications are erected as from the 8th century. Although few remains of buildings were found, the tombs and graves revealed rich finds.

The Cinyrad family continued to rule as Kings and the High Priests of **WANASSA** (The Lady) as Aphrodite was then known. The festivals of Aphrodite were the centre of the annual activity of the city and included also great cultural events. Homer wrote his *"Hymn to Aphrodite"* describing such events.

Syllabic script was developed and widely used. Coins were minted. Despite foreign occupation by Assyrians and Egyptians, the kingdom had a great degree of Independence.

The Persians occupied Cyprus in 545; the kingdom of Paleapaphos continued with its religious and political freedom.

The Remains of the Sugar Mills.

THE SIEGE OF PALEAPAPHOS

In 499BC the *"Ionian Revolt"* in Asia Minor and Cyprus started against Persian rule. Paleapaphos strengthened its defences in anticipation of Persian attacks. The Persian armies defeated the Greeks. In Cyprus, the Phoenician elements and kingdoms sided with the Persians — this influenced the outcome. In quick succession the rebellious kingdoms of Cyprus were defeated. In Paleapaphos a long siege started in 498BC. A mound (a bank of earth or stones) was built by the Persians on the *North East Gate - Marcello Hill.* Buildings, Temples and Statues outside the walls were destroyed and used for the building of the mound.

Such fragments were recently discovered in large quantities including a fine head of a Priest King, a Bronze Helmet   hundreds of spear and arrow heads, limestone figures and inscriptions.

Tunnels were constructed by defenders to undermine the mound and they removed as much material as possible. The mining of such tunnels was formidable; they were then filled with wood, set alight and the mound collapsed.

However, despite the heroic defences, the superiority of the Persians succeeded in overrunning the town by storm; there is an absence of the final events — although the actual siege is well documented.

CLASSICAL PERIOD 475-325BC.

Despite the harsh Persian rule, the Cinyra Kings retained some influence and continued to mint their own coins. Recorded kings included *Penthylos* and *Timochare* At first the walls remained unattended although large buildings were erected. The surviving PALACE at Hadji Abdulla area is a fine building believed to have housed either the king or the Persia governor. Large limestone blocks were used for the walls.

Although no remains of the Classic Temple remain, the cult of Aphrodi continued and Paphos remained the cent of worshipping. Economic activity w booming.

Paleapaphos, together with all the oth Cypriot Kingdoms declared support an assistance to Alexander the Great 331BC. This change of events affected th Kingdom of Paleapaphos more than an other in the island.

HELLENISTIC PERIOD 325-58B

The last king to serve at Paleapaphos w **NICOCLES.** In c. 320BC he transferre the seat of government to Nea Paph which was established as a port. He was a enterprising monarch who built temp and buildings in Nea Paphos but al strengthened the Sanctuary of Aphrodit Paleapaphos retained its Religious impo tance. Cyprus came under the dominati of the Greek rulers of Egypt th

PTOLEMIES who established Nea Paphos as their administrative centre of the island. The Cinyrad family continued their role as the High Priests of the sanctuary and a new lease of life was given by the new rulers. Queen Arsinoe, sister of Ptolemy Philadelphus was introduced by her brother into the cult.

ROMAN PERIOD 58BC-330AD — Palea-

paphos saw a change under the Romans. The cult of Aphrodite, goddess of Fertility, gradually changed to VENUS, goddess of Love. The mysteries had more sexual and lustful connotations.

Paleapaphos became a very important religious centre attracting thousands of visitors annually from all over the Empire. Visitors continued to disembark at Nea Paphos harbour, crowned with myrtle and accompanied with music started a procession to the sanctuary. Events included games, music, dancing and poetry.

New buildings were erected and coins were minted showing the sanctuary with the conical stone, symbol of fertility. Emperor Titus recorded that he visited Paleapaphos in 69AD.

The earthquake of 15BC inflicted severe damage but eventually the sanctuary was rebuilt with funds provided by Emperor Augustus. Finds from tombs of the Roman period indicate that very wealthy Roman families lived and were buried here.

A mosaic floor was found in one Roman villa, that of LEDA. It was housed at the Kouklia museum, it was then stolen and found in Europe, brought back to Cyprus and now is on display at the Cyprus Museum. It shows beautiful Leda from the back teasing amorous Zeus who is disguised as a swan; a fine mosaic.

EARLY BYZANTINE PERIOD 330-

641AD. Christianity was a turning point to the Roman Empire and also for Paleapaphos. The newly established church objected strongly to the continuity of the rites, although the strength of the cult strongly resisted any changes during the early years; it was finally outlawed by Emperor Theodosios in 391AD.

Neglect and nature destroyed the sanctuary after 14 centuries of continuous activity.

MEDIEVAL-FRANKISH RULE – It

was not until the 12th century AD that Paleapaphos known as COUVOUCLE (KOUKLIA) attracted the Lusignan rulers — thanks to its surrounding fertile land. A Royal manor was built on the southern site of the Temple from which stones were used. Nearby, a small but interesting church, KATHOLIKI CHURCH, served the Latin community. Kouklia became the commercial centre of Paphos with the production and the refinery of SUGAR, an extremely important commodity in those days. Ruins of the sugar cane mill refinery were recently found south of the Manor and the main Paphos-Limassol road.

All secondary sites are fenced. The Temple is open to the public and a fee is required to enter the Manor and the Museum.

Detailed of the site of the North East Gate — *Marcello Hill* and the siege mount. Most excavated work is now covered with grass. The area is fenced.

PETRA TOU ROMIOU
(Aphrodite's Birthplace)

On reaching Petra Tou Romiou one can see impressive rock formations, with the largest rock close to the beach. If one walks along the beach on either side of the rock, a strange feeling may overcome him. Going up hill once you pass the rock and stopping by the side of the road, there is a beautiful view of the rock, the bay and the surrounding area. According to Greek mythology Aphrodite was born here. She rose from the white foam of the soft waves, floated on a sea shell and came to rest at Paleapaphos, where her Temple was erected.

In his Odyssey VIII, 362 Homer wrote:
"But laugher-loving Aphrodite went to Cyprus, to Paphos, in her precinct and fragrant altars. . ."

"The moist breeze of zephyr brought her there (to Paphos' shores) on the waves of the sea, with a noise of thunder, among the soft foam, and the gold-dressed Horä (beautiful women priestesses) received her with joy. They decked her with valuable jewels and on her immortal head they placed a beautiful gold crown and in her ears two earrings of copper and gold. . ."

For swimmers this is an ideal place, since the sea is usually very calm and the beach is sandy in places although on the eastern side there are pebbles. On the western side undercurrents occur and the water can get very deep. Nearby there is a restaurant and cafeteria run by the Tourist Organisation where one can eat and obtain refreshments. It is open all day and part of the night, and provides a very good view of the rock and the beach below. It is worth waiting here for the sunset which is beautiful.

3 different views of "Petra tou Romiou" or Aphrodite's Birthplace as is commonly known, where according to the legend the Goddess of Love was born from the foam of the sea.

THE PRIESTESSES OF APHRODITE IN ANCIENT PAPHOS

by *STASS PARASKOS*

Senior Lecturer — Canterbury College of Art

One of the most famous kings of ancient Cyprus was Cinyras who reigned in Paphos at the time of the Trojan War. He was a Phoenician prince who went to Cyprus with a band of followers seeking new homes because there was famine in their own country. They landed on the west coast of Cyprus near where the goddess Aphrodite had first set foot when she rose from the waves. The area was fertile and they were well content to settle there. So they built themselves a town, and in the centre of it erected a temple to Aphrodite, who, they believed, had guided them to her birthplace, and Cinyras became the first king and high priest of the new city, which they named Paphos in honour of his mother. For over a thousand years the Temple had remained a centre of worship and a meeting place for people of the Eastern Mediterranean; its fame ensuring that the goddess of Love would forever be associated with Paphos.

Cinyras had introduced sacred "prostitution" as part of the cult of Aphrodite and the temple in Paphos was famous for the large number of its beautiful priestesses. There were precedents for this, for in ancient times prostitution was a profession free of social or moral stigma. Indeed it was believed to fulfil social and educational needs and municipal brothels thrived throughout the ancient world. Many public figures, including the great Athenian statesman Pericles were associated with prostitutes and the famous courtesan Phryne was commemorated with a statue at Delphi, the most sacred place in all Greece. The religious aspect of harlotry was based on the belief that anyone having intercourse with a priestess of the goddess of procreation would be rewarded with prosperity.

The priestesses of Aphrodite in Paphos, were trained in the complex rules of sacrifice, prayer and purification. They played prominent parts during the Aphrodisia festival and took part in sacrificial feasts. When public prayers were offered to the goddess their participation in large numbers was considered essential. Priestesses were not required to possess any special qualities other than the willingness to carry out their duties

conscientiously. Some self-employed prostitutes worked part-time in the temple and were allowed to keep part of the money they had earned there.

The usual source of prospective priestesses was the lowest class of temple ministrants, called the sacred servants. Some of these servants were bought by the temple, others were dedicated to it by their parents when they were children. Their numbers ran into thousands of both sexes and all were at the High Priest's beck and call. Normally they would be put to domestic or agricultural work, but some of the women were creamed off and trained as priestesses.

Another source of priestesses were the wealthy pilgrims with their slave girls. In those times men always sought to gain the affection of their gods through bribery and to this effect the rich bought beautiful girls and dedicated them to Aphrodite. In return the goddess was expected to repay the kindness shown to her and for this reason, at the end of the dedication ceremony, the donors stood up with arms outstretched and palms turned expectantly upwards as though in the act of receiving a present.

Roman Coin showing the sanctuary of Aphrodite. *(Courtesy Cyprus Museum)*

All women in Paphos had to serve in the temple for one day a year during a festival called the Aphrodisia, celebrating the reunion of Aphrodite with her lover Adonis who returned from the dead at the beginning of every spring. The daughters of king Cinyras also served the goddess in this way — an indication that the rule embraced all women of a certain age, irrespective of social class.

The girls wore special head scarves and sat in a line at the entrance of the great temple waiting to be chosen by a man. Men paraded up and down inspecting the girls and when one of them took their fancy they threw a silver coin in her lap and claimed her in the name of the goddess. The girls had no right to refuse a man and the silver coin went to the temple. The idea behind this rite was to imitate the reunion of Aphrodite with Adonis. For the same reason a sacred marriage between the High Priest, representing Adonis, and a priestess, representing Aphrodite, was performed in the Temple and was consummated in a chamber decorated with greenery. These rites pleased the goddess of fertility who responded by activating the creative forces of nature so that the crops grew and the animals were able to reproduce their kind.

In early antiquity, when women in Paphos were still forbidden to marry unless they had first had intercourse with a stranger, all girls had to act as priestesses temporarily, until they were relieved of their maidenhood. In those days Cypriot men considered the act of deflowering a virgin dangerous and the temples of Aphrodite became crowded with girls waiting for foreign pilgrims. It is not surprising that some women waited for years before they attracted a lover.

It is wrong to assume that all the temples of Aphrodite were palaces of licence and debauchery and that all her priestesses were part-time prostitutes. It must be remembered that Aphrodite was not only the goddess of love but also the guardian of women in vulnerable positions, the protectress of innocence in young girls, she guarded over the sanctity of marriage and had powers to produce rain and calm the sea. There were temples dedicated to Aphrodite where the priestesses had to be virgins and if any of them broke her vows of chastity she was punished severely. On one occasion a priestess was buried alive. Men who accused a virgin priestess of Aphrodite without justification were charged before a priest-judge who could sentence them to have their foreheads branded.

The office of the high priest was not open to women but some priestesses, with special intuitive talents, rose to become oracles of the temple. These girls, being the main channel through which the goddess spoke, were extremely influential and were consulted by government officials and the military, as well as by private citizens. They spoke in the name of Aphrodite after having been stimulated by some device into an ecstatic condition. The knowledge that matters of life and death depended on their advice ensured that oracles would take their duties seriously. The vagueness of some of their answers was not designed merely to cover themselves in case of failure but was due also to their reluctance to commit themselves lightly. If one is to judge from their popularity, they seemed to have exercised their duties well and to the benefit of those who sought their advice.

Further reading: APHRODITE and the Mythology of Cyprus — by STASS PARASKOS is published by Interworld and is on sale in both Cyprus and the U.K.

Petra tou Romiou Rocks

ROUTE A-2 **TO ARKHIMANDRITA**

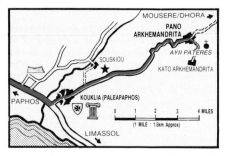

Some six to seven miles north east of Kouklia is the village of **Pano Arkhimandrita.** The drive is easy and the road wide, the scenery, like most other places of Paphos is constantly changing and breathtaking. The village is built at the top of a plateaux and about ¼ of a mile below to the south is the old site of **Kato Arkhimandrita.** There are about 300 inhabitants in the village, mainly farmers, but like most of the villages, it has empty houses as

people emigrated to the towns or abroad. The village church has interesting icons of the 16th century in Cretan-Cypriote style.

Near Kato Arkhimandrita is the *Hermitage of Ayii Pateras* (Holy Fathers) and is inside a rock cut tomb believed to be of Roman origin. Some bones were kept in the cave in special places. A local story explains that the place is holy due to the slaughter of over 300 Christian refugees who came here from the persecutions in Syria, only to find an end to their lives from local people who objected to their presence.

For those with time on their hands and who like hard, slow driving in winding unsurfaced roads, further excursions to **Mousere** and **Dhora** (a village with an interesting church) will provide scenic views. After Dhora, the road is again good and for the return trip you go to Malia and from there either north to circle around Arsos — Ayios Nicolaos — Kedhares — Mamonia — Nikoklia or via Pakhna (going south), Prastio and Evdhimou.

Two views of Arkhimandrita village.

MOUNTAIN EXCURSIONS
ROUTES B-1, B-2, B-3, B-4, B-5

These trips will take you high up into the mountains, to the edge of the Troodos Mountain Range, where the forest is very interesting. The road up to Panayia is good and wide most of the way and passes through some old and famous vineyards. The aim of the trip is to visit Khrysorroyiatissa Monastery (26 miles from Paphos); or the famous Cedar Valley and Stavros tis Psokas. The return trip could be by the same route; or one could make the return journey by carrying on through Pentalia and Amargeti, although this route is very twisting and requires more care. However, the scenery is breath-taking. One could even take this route first and return the other way. Whatever one decides, this is a worth-while journey.

Selladhi tou Stavrou

STAVROS
TIS PSOKAS

STAVROS

Dodeka
Anemi

DASOS PAPHOU
(PAPHOS FOREST)

KYKKO MON

Xeropiyi

Moummouros

Selladhi tou
Aphoriti

Moutti tou
Kourkouta

AYIA

KILADA KEDRON
(CEDAR VALLEY)

LYSOS

STAVROS
TOU
KRATIMATOU

SARAMA

ANADIOU

PHITI

KRITOU
MARROTTOU

ASPROYIA

KANNAVIOU

PANAYIA

AYIOS DEMETRIANOS

KHRYSORROYIATISSA MON.

AYIA MONI

MELADIOU

LAPITHIOU

POLIS

PSATHI

STATOS

STROUMBI

POLEMI

KILINIA

AYIOS PHOTIOS

GALATARIA

Ayi

Kremmos
Triantaphyllo

PENDALIA

TSADA

Moronero

AYIA MARINA

AMARGETI

POTAMOS TIS EZOUSAS

Lofos
Axylou

ELEDHIOU

AXYLOU

XEROS POTAMOS

PAPHOS

NATA

KHOLETRIA

ANARITA

PHINIKAS

TIMI

0 1 2 3 4 5 MILES

(1 MILE = 1.5km Approx)

LIMASSOL

The Church of Khrysorroyiatissa Monastery.

A field with Flowers. Spring in Paphos is a paradise
(Courtesy Stephanos Theodorou)

The Guests quarters of Khrysorroyiatissa Monastery.

Residential Buildings at Ayia Moni where guests can stay. In this area there are plans to build a cultural centre which will be a major attraction to both visitors and local people.

POLEMI, PSATHI AND AYIOS DEMETRIANOS

Leaving the main road from Paphos to Polis, after the village of Tsada, you turn right and go through Polemi, Psathi and Ayios Demetrianos. Near Polemi in the spring you can admire the wild tulips scattered over the fields. These are basically wine centres and, after driving through the vineyards, olive groves and almond trees, you reach **Kannaviou,** which is merely a stopping point where one can rest and relax under the enormous trees in the coolness of the valley. Cafeterias will serve refreshments and food.

Route B-1 to the Monastery of Khrysorroyiatissa

PANAYIA

This is an interesting village, the largest in the region, built on the side of hills amongst vineyards, apple trees and pine trees. It is well known as it was here that the late Archbishop Makarios III was born and spent his childhood as a shepherd. His original home is well-preserved and open for the public to view. The Church of Panayia is also of interest.

MONASTERY OF KHRYSORROYIATISSA

This is a very delightful monastery, built on the side of Royia mountain, some 2768 feet high with a wonderful view of the surrounding valleys and villages. It was founded in 1152 AD by a monk called Ignatius. He also discovered the miraculous icon of the Virgin Mary, which was painted by St. Luke The Evangelist. The legend says that the icon was thrown into the sea during the Iconoclastic Wars in Isauria and was washed up on the beach of Moulia, near Yeroskipos, along the coast of Paphos.

A fisherman kept it in a cave nearby where it was found four Centuries later by the monk Ignatius. The Franks, and then the Turks, persecuted the monastery and it was only in

53

Above: View of Panayia village. Below: Khrysorroyiatissa monastery.

CEDAR VALLEY

You may reach this unique area of the Cyprus forest after visiting Stavros tis Psokas; or just before arriving at the village of Panayia, you take the mountain road towards the valley. The main characteristic of the forest is that most of the trees are CEDARS. From the area of Stavros to the Valley of Cedars you may be lucky enough to catch a glimpse of the national animal of Cyprus —**the Mouflon** — a wild but friendly animal belonging to the sheep family. This shy yet elegant animal will usually be spotted in the early morning or late afternoon.

From the Cedar Valley you can reach the Kykko Monastery situated in the most idyllic forest. The monastery is in the Nicosia district.

The Cedar Valley *(Courtesy Cyprus Tourism Organisation)*

the 18th Century that it was allowed to function freely. It was at this time that most of the buildings were erected. Abbots were ordained from 1770 AD. During the Greek mainland revolution of 1821 the monastery had shown some resistance against the Turks, and it was soon to be occupied by the Turkish army and suffered much damage. Abbott Kyrillos Georgiades managed to revive it in later times. In 1967 a fire destroyed most

A stamp of Europa 1978 issue showing the monastery of Khrysorroyiatissa

of the monastery, but it was restored soon afterwards. Around the monastery there are plantations of apple trees, cherry trees. etc.

Inside the picturesque church there are treasures and beautiful icons, the most famous being that of The Virgin Mary Khrysorroyiatissa (18th Century). The monastery has an interesting collection of Holy Gospels, books of religious music, manuscripts, religious ornaments and crosses. Overnight accommodation is available and during the summer you are advised to contact the monastery beforehand to secure a vacancy. There is also a restaurant and cafeteria, with spectacular views over the valley.

AYIA MONI

Ayia Moni is less than 2 miles south of the monastery of **Khrysorroyiatissa.** The church, one of the oldest in Cyprus being established in the 4th century A.D. was erected on the site of an ancient and important Temple, that of **Hera.** Some inscriptions were found among the foundations in the Cypriote Character and other places, in ancient Greek. The church is dedicated to *St. Nickolas.* The monastery buildings, some dating to 1638 and 1820 are in partial restoration. They form a "U" shape and have a courtyard. A family runs a taverna — cafeteria and refreshments and meals are served mainly during the spring and summer.

Ayia Moni is situated in a unique and very favourable spot, the right choice for a temple and a monastic retreat. The cliffs of *Aetokremmos* mountain surround it from 3 sides forming a half moon shape, thus averting every wind except from the west side. A spring, famous through the district for its purity, runs below providing water and greenery.

Profitis Elias, a small chapel high up the mountain of *Ayia* some 2 miles east of Khrysorroyiatissa mon. and north east of Ayia Moni is of no great interest except for its unique scenic views. It is situated on the highest spot and dedicated to Profitis Elias, the Saint of rain, thunder and lightning. You can reach this place on foot only, ideal for country walkers and explorers.

In times of long periods of drought, people used to gather at the monastery of Khrysorroyiatissa and process the icon of The Virgin to Ayia Moni (ruined chapel of Ayios Efthymios) and from there climb up the mountain to the chapel of Profitis Elias for prayers.

Route B-2 to the Forest
STAVROS TIS PSOKAS

After Kannaviou you take the road towards Stavros tis Psokas: this is an interesting valley in a beautiful forest. Situated 33 miles from Paphos, this is the main rest area of the forest where beds are available in log cabins for a minimal charge. If you wish to stay and explore this lovely forest, telephone the Forestry Department in Nicosia, telephone 40-2264, to reserve accommodation.

Please remember that although the distance is short in miles it is long in driving time, as the road up to the mountains is twisting and narrow.

This impressive stamp of the definitive issue of 1962 shows the Mouflon the lovable animal not only in Paphos but in the whole of Cyprus
Courtesy, Cyprus Philatelic Bureaux

In 1907 the late Sir Winston Churchill, as Under Secretary of State for the Colonies, visited Cyprus and was appalled by the state of the forest. He requested extra funds, of which most went to Stavros tis Psokas which was already, established as a forest station (1884). Now it is the headquarters of the forestry department controlling some 2/3rds of all Cyprus' Forests which we all enjoy and which plays such a great part in the island's economy.

THE FOREST OF PAPHOS

The forest of Paphos, arguably the most beautiful in the Middle East, covers most of the north-eastern part of Paphos stretching into the Western Nicosia district. For the most part it is not easily accessible. The existing roads are narrow and generally unsurfaced so make sure that you have good transport.

Above and *left:* Two views of the Paphos Forest.
Below: Stavros tis Psokas forestry station.

Stavros tis Psokas provides excellent and panoramic views of the surrounding areas. Picnic sites are well established with special areas allocated for barbeque and souvla next to running cool water. The cafe restaurant close to the forestry station provides basic meals and snacks.

Route B-3
via Statos to Timi

Should you wish to return via this route you will enjoy nice scenery and picturesque villages and the valleys of the rivers Ezousas and Xeros Potamos.

STATOS

This is the first village you reach after Ayia Moni. It is famous for its Cypriot food specialities known to lovers of **"Meze"** as **Loukanika** (a kind of spicy sausage) and **Lountza** (smoked pork meat). In the surrounding area some monolithic stones were observed by past travellers together with traces of old habitation.

To the south there is a road junction and the small village of **AYIOS PHOTIOS.**

Route B-4

For those who enjoy tiring but adventurous driving compensated with scenic views, a trip to the east and the surrounding areas would be enjoyable. First you reach **GALATARIA,** a small village with an interesting church and then to **KILINIA.**

From here the road becomes unsurfaced and difficult and the country side almost deserted. After the hamlets of **VRESHA**

you reach the narrow gorge of the *Ezousas river* and the *Roudhias Bridge,* of Venetian origin. Here in the locality according to the British explorer D.G. Hogarth - 1888: "There is a mill and in the ground and near the mill a sculptured stele representing 2 female and a male figures. The clumsy lines of the drapery recall the statuettes found in Amargeti. The interest of the stele is that there are no known ancient sites in the area. Who then brought this heavy stele here and why?".

Further to the east is the abandoned settlement of **PERAVASA** and the old bridge of *Kelephos.* These truck roads were old camel routes. Then you reach, in the south, either Arminou or Ayios Nicolaos and from there back to Paphos on a good road (see route H).

Back to our main route B-3

PENDALIA

There is an interesting church here with old icons. Ancient tombs were found by the side of the chalky cliff overlooking the village and also to the south.

AMARGETI

This village has a fascinating church with some good icons. This is also a village with an old history, not only for its medieval settlements but for settlements dating back to the Bronze Age. There are some ruins of the Temple dedicated to **Apollo Melanthius** (the healer of the sick) which dates back to 400 BC. A great number of small objects including doves, statuettes, phalic objects, cones, bunches of grapes etc were found in the area and also inscriptions with strange dedications; all were discovered by D.H. Hogarth in 1887-88.

Amargeti village with its interesting church

ELEDHIOU - AXYLOU - NATA

As with the other villages, the main occupation of the people is farming and agriculture with vineyards, almonds, carrobs, olives some citrus and cattle.

ANARITA

This village enjoys the honour of originating **HALLOUMI** cheese (the famous Cypriot goat cheese) since **"Anari"** is the condensed whey which is produced by a by-product when making the cheese. Every May the *"Halloumi Festival"* is held here. To the south are the remains of the monastery of *Ayios Onesiforos* of Byzantine times.

TIMI

Close to the main Paphos-Limassol road (northern side), Timi is becoming important not only as an agricultural centre, but also due to the establishment of the International Airport a few miles to the south. In the village, signs have been found of an early Bronze age civilization, also of Greek and Roman settlements. As in most other villages, the church is worth seeing.

Timi is also known for its delicious Loukanika sausages and goats cheese (halloumi).

Reaching the main road, carefully turn right and drive back to Paphos town.

Above: General view of Anarita village (photo: Stephanos Theodorou). Below: The church and square of Phiti village. The monument to the left is erected by the villagers to those who emigrated to foreign lands but did not forget their origin and with funds helped the village by bringing water

58

Route B-5 to Phiti

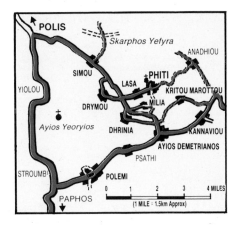

From **Ayios Demitrianos** (see route B1) you turn to the west and after a short drive a left turning will take you to **DHRINIA**, a small village, but if you continue you pass south of **MILIA** and reach **LASA**, another village with a modern church. All these 3 villages and the surrounding countryside, are picturesque, and best seen during spring.

From Lasa, turn right and you reach **PHITI** with old, usually empty houses and narrow streets. It is famed for its embroidery, unique to the Paphos area. Local women weave and embroider beautiful items which are worth purchasing. Please consult someone at the cafe in the square. Phiti is also famous for its **"moonshine"** — an alcoholic spirit called **Zivania** which is over 90 % strong (pure spirit) and is exported to Russia for making Vodka; it is made from the remains of grapes that have been already used for making wine. The church in the main square is again of some interest.

For your return journey you can proceed to **DHRYMOU** westward whose church is interesting. Some ancient ruins were discovered here, believed to be of a **Temple of Apollo Hylates** but apart from some megalithic stones there isn't much to be seen.

Further west is **SIMOU** a very nice agricultural village. From here you may attempt over a truck road to visit the gorge of *Potamos tou Stavrou tis Psokas* and the old bridge of *Skarphos* and explore the remote countryside.

Back at Simou, you continue your journey through absorbing countryside and you reach the main road Paphos — Polis. If you have time to spare, you turn right towards Polis or turn left for Paphos, only a 20 minute drive.

Route C-1 to Khoulou - Vineyards of Paphos

Along the main Paphos-Polis road you turn right into the village of **TSADA** (about 900 inh.). From here you will enjoy a Panoramic view of the coastline from Coral Bay to Yeroskipos, and admire the town of Paphos and the harbour. There is a church in the village which was rebuilt in 1908 containing an icon of the Virgin dating to 1540, with the following inscription:

> **"Accept O All Holy Virgin the prayer of the servant the Priest Gideon and his wife and place them in the land of the just. This icon was painted at the expense and by the hand of Titus the Sinner".**

After the village continue along the road and turn left going north to **KALLEPIA** which has a church with a reputation and appearance of a great age. To the north east are the ruins of a monastery.

LETYMBOU — An interesting village known for its numerous churches scattered all over the area including *St. Kyriakos* with its numerous frescoes, *Ayios Theodoros* and *Panayia Photolambousa.* During the Lusignan Frankish period, Letymbou played a prominent role as a centre of local government and it also had a court. Old style village houses abound in the vicinity.

Much of Paphos countryside is covered with well looked after vines which with modern methods of cultivation produce excellent grapes for wine.

Stavros tis Mythras monastery and surrounding vineyards (photo: Stephanos Theodorou)

Above: View of Dhrinia village. Below: General view of Episkopi village. (photos: Stephanos Theodorou)

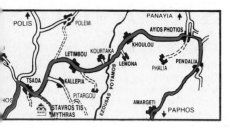

Crossing the valley of the *Ezousas river* and the small villages of **KOURTALA** and **LEMONA** you reach **KHOULOU.** The village is of no great importance but the surrounding area is nice. It is a centre of vineyards, citrus, vegetables, tobacco and potatoes.

From here you can proceed through a different road to the junction of **Ayios Photios** and go through to Khrysorroyiatissa mon. to the north (route B1) or southward via Timi (route B3). This route is for those who love exploring and have already visited most other places, as it is of no great importance; however you may wish to make the return trip to Khrysorroyiatissa monastery through here.

Route C-2
STAVROS TIS MYTHRAS

This small monastery can be reached from **Tsada** which is about 2 miles. It is situated south east of the village. It is part of a large property which is administered by the See of Paphos and served at one time as the official residence of the Bishop. The buildings provide some guest rooms and some of the doorways distinctly show a unique Gothic style. The present church is dated 1740. A text in ancient Cypriot writing was found here. In the monastery there is a large cross which was covered once with silver. Around 1834 there was a fierce fire in the monastery and an abbot seized the cross and threw it into the flames. The silver melted and extinguished the fire and some signs of the burning can be seen on the cross. The surrounding area is full of vineyards.

Route C-3
to Episkopi

This is a short but very interesting scenic journey for an afternoon or morning outing. Go through the north east part of Paphos town and pass the Youth Hostel (Eleftherios Venizelos Avenue). After a short drive, on the left there is a road going to **ANAVARGOS** and then to the right is **KONIA,** a very popular place for British people to settle. They enjoy panoramic views of the coastline.

Further up there is a crossroad. To the left is **ARMOU** where there are some tombs and remains of a Roman villa. Panoramic views of Paphos. To the right is **MARATHOUNDHA.** There are ruined churches in the countryside. The church of the village is interesting and there is a limestone altar with large letters in script of the Ptolemaic period "*Apolloni Myrati Xanthos Ipper Onasa Viskon*". Signs of a Temple were found believed to be that of Apollo.

EPISKOPI

About 10 miles from Paphos. Situated by the fertile valley of the *Ezousas river* and provides beautiful views. Late Roman remains were

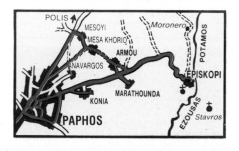

found here. This, together with other places of Roman settlements, prove that not only Nea Paphos and the coastal area were inhabited by Romans and earlier peoples, but their settlements were spread all over the countryside.

There is a 12-13th cent. church which is of some interest, dedicated to *Ayios Hilarion* who came here from Palestine where he introduced monastic life, and spent his last years in a cave which is outside the village. According to St. Jerome "*. . . he entered Paphos, that city of Cyprus so nobly celebrated by the poets, which destroyed by frequent earthquakes, has now only its ruins to show that once it was . . .*"

When St. Hilarion died in Episkopi he was buried here but his followers stole the corpse and took it back to Palestine.

AYIOS NEOPHITOS MONASTERY

This is a short trip to the famous monastery of Ayios Neophitos. To reach the monastery, one turns left at Mesoyi village and follows the road through the neighbouring small village of Trimithousa, which was once an estate given in 1375 AD to Sir Theobald Belfarage by King Peter II, for his services against the Genoese invaders.

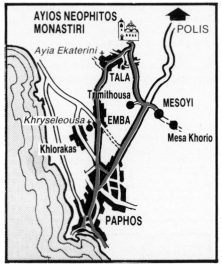

AYIOS NEOPHITOS MONASTERY

This is an impressive collection of buildings, with a courtyard and church in the centre. Adjoining the monastery there is a restaurant built into the side of the hill, just above the village of Tala. Taking the climb to the top of the hill one is able to enjoy the fantastic view over the valley below, looking towards the villages of Emba, Kissonerga and even as far as the Coral Bay area. The view takes in all the surrounding area, right down to the coast.

The monastery was founded by Ayios Neophitos, one of the most important Saints in Cyprus. He arrived in Paphos around 1159 AD. He cut three caves from the rock at the side of the hill, far above the ground, giving him shelter and security and he stayed there as a hermit. Steps lead up to the cave, which is called Enclistra. There are

Wall painting of Christ the Pantocrator (the Creator of All) from the Enclistra wall paintings.

Fresco of the Three Saints which is in the church.

Apart from the superb wall paintings of the Englistra the visitor can enjoy interesting wall paintings inside the Church where are also to be seen wood-carvings. The sacred skull of the Saint is kept inside a silver case and has a pyramid-shaped cover. The wooden-carved Iconostasi displays very artistic Icons. More treasures can be seen in the small museum of the monastery.

many frescoes, some executed under the supervision of the Saint himself, which are in very good condition and are to be admired. Other frescoes in the cave were painted around the 15th Century. These are:

The Enclistra where Ayios Neophitos used to live. The wall paintings are in the lower part.

AYIOS NEOPHITOS — Icon of St. Mark dating to the 15th cent.

View of Ayios Neophitos monastery from the Enclistra.

In The Nave
Abraham and Three Angels (south wall)
A Group of Various Saints (west wall)
Subjects from The New Testament (upper wall)
St. Helena and Constantine The Great (east wall)

In The Bema
Various Saints — Ephraim, Hilarion, Theodoros (north and west walls)
The Prayer of Prophesis (east wall)
Christ The Pantokrator (roof)
The Ascension (ceiling)
St. Neophytos between The Archangels Gabriel and Michael, who lead him to Christ on the Day of Judgement.

In The Cell
Further frescoes can be seen here. This is the place where the Saint used to sleep and measures only 8 feet by 11 feet. The Saint also had a library and stone table in this room.

The main buildings around the church, some of them built more recently, are used by the monks as living quarters. There is also some space where visitors can stay overnight.

The Church
This building, interesting from the outside, is even more interesting on the inside, with frescoes and paintings in pure Byzantine style. They are all stated to be 15th Century.

The Icons in the Church of Avios Neophitos

The icons which cover the iconostasi are also worth seeing, as too are the carved wooden statues.

The Church is dedicated to The Virgin Mary, although the name of Ayios Neophitos is given to the church by many people.

The whole area around the monastery has enormous beauty and is surrounded by vineyards, trees, gardens and running water. It is a very popular place and visited by many people, so if one would prefer to visit at a quiet time, a visit at the beginning of the week rather than weekends would be recommended.

Biography of The Saint
Ayios Neophitos was born near Lefkara in the village of Kato-Dris (Limassol — Larnaca area) in 1134 AD. When he was 18 he entered the monastery of Ayios Chrysostomos and here he learned to read and write. He visited the Holy Places in Jerusalem, but on his return to Cyprus he decided to find a place that was quiet to rest his life and soul in isolation. He at last arrived at this monastery, which he created. Whilst in isolation he wrote many hymns and books dedicated to The Virgin Mary, Holy Cross and Jesus Christ. He also wrote the Fifty Chapter Bible. Also famous is the letter in which he describes the occupation of Cyprus by Richard Coeur de Lion, entitled "Concerning the Misfortunes of Cyprus". During the latter years of his life he attracted fame and many people came to listen to his teachings. Many people who came wanted to help and became monks.

In 1170 AD his work was honoured by the Bishop of Paphos, Basil Kinnamos, who ordained him as a priest. He died around 1219, at the age of 85 (or thereabouts).

Many of his manuscripts survive today and in the monastery there is a workshop which is restoring all that is left and binding it into books.

The discovery of Ayios Neophitos Tomb.
When Cyprus was occupied by the Turks in 1571, the monks of the monastery sealed off the Enclistra and the saints tomb and painted a frescoe to conceal the door and over and around it where it can be seen now. It was re-discovered some 200 years later in 1757 as follows: A monk of the monastery, believing that there was treasure inside the Enclistra, discovered the sealed door and one night broke it open and to his surprise found a tomb. While he was attempting to remove the stone covering it he was suddenly struck down by a mysterious force. When he recovered his senses, he rushed to see the abbot and told him of his discovery. Early in the morning the abbot and the monks went to the Enkleistra and saw the tomb and inside the grave found the body of Ayios Neophitos clad in the garments which he had himself woven and girt with the iron girdle which he had worn during his lifetime.

Leaving the monastery you may return to Paphos via Tala and Emba. The road goes through the hills where a modern village is growing with new villas that have beautiful views of the coastline. It is popular with British families who have settled here.

TALA is in contrast to the modern village. You go through the narrow main roads with its old houses. To the west of the square is the church of *Ayia Ekaterini*. About 3 miles to the northwest of the village an early Cypriote cemetary was found recently.

EMBA is a large village with about 1000 inhabitants. Spring is an ideal time to enjoy the countryside around the village with fields full of wild flowers and cyclamen. The word *Emba* means *Entrance* and it was, in fact, the western entrance to Paphos. It was an important place during the Frankish period and was one of the 5 Bailiwicks into which the Paphos district was divided.

The church of the *Virgin Mary Khryseleousa* is of great importance and dates to the 13th century with later additions. There are beautiful icons and the frescoe of the New Testament, but unfortunately, most of the other frescoes have been very cruelly restored.

To the south of the village is the small chapel of *Ayios Limpros* and a cave called *Petridia* which is natural and has stalactites. The water is believed to cure a variety of skin diseases.

Above: EMBA-Wall painting in the church of Panayia Mary Khryseleousa representing the miracle of fishing 15th cent. AD.
Below: The church of Panayia Mary Khryseleousa is of fine Byzantine architecture.

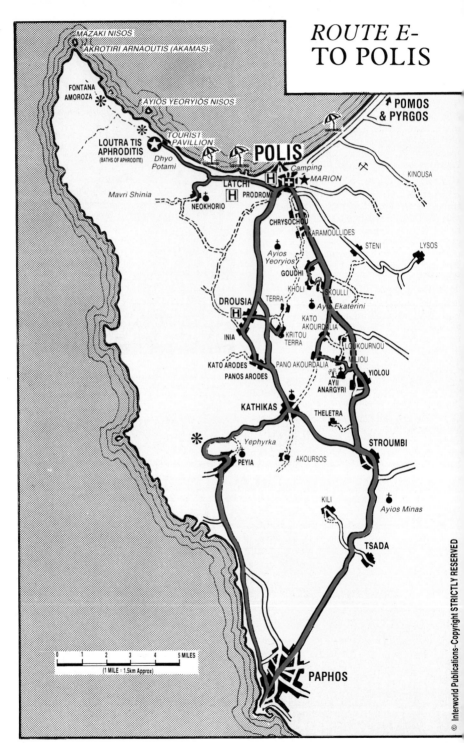

ROUTE E-
TO POLIS

There are two routes to Polis and the Baths of Aphrodite and you may go one way and return the other, thus making the trip more interesting as the roads are very good. In fact, there is a third route going along the coastal road towards Coral Bay, then turning to Peyia and from there via Arodhes.

Route E-1 Via Yiolou

To the left of the junction to **TSADA** (see route C-1) you go towards **KILI**, a small village commanding a panoramic view of the coastline. There is the chapel of *Ayios Mamas* above the village and to the south is *Ayia Varvara* chapel. Other chapels are in ruins. There are also caves *(Kyra Vrisi)* but take much care if you risk entering them.

Pass Tsada and reach **STROUMBI** with about 700 inh. This is a famous vineyard centre producing excellent wine and mentioned by Lawrence Durrell in his book about life in Cyprus *"Bitter Lemons"*. A Frankish Estate was established here.

THELEDRA is to the left of the main road, on the side of a hill. The church dated 1755 has interesting icons. Local women produce good embroidery but in the past it was known as the ideal place for shepherds to bring their sheep during the summer months due to the existence of vegetation, thus the name was given *"Golden Theledra"*. Around the area are traces of Neolithic settlements and ruins of a medieval church.

YIOLOU — Another wine centre. Its 19th century church is of interest. The surrounding area and in the hills up to Theledra is wonderful during the spring, full of beautiful flowers called Matsikorida.

AYII ANARGYRI. An old monastic complex, built around 1649 believed to be on the site of a stone age settlement. It was founded by the brothers Cosmas and Damianos, an unmercenary duo who gave their services to the poor. Now it is a centre for Mineral Baths due to its famous therapeutic waters. The sulphur baths are helpful to many ailments, including rheumatism, arthritis, spinal problems, gastritis ulcers etc. There is also a small hotel.

A short diversion will take you from here west towards **MILIOU** where traces of old habitation were found, then north to Pano and Kato **AKOURDALIA** with interesting scenery and a nice church, then back to the main road.

LOUKOURNOU, SKOULLI, KHOLI are to the left of the main road by the side of hills. Citrus trees are to be seen in the narrow gorges. **KHOLI** has a beautiful church, that of *Arkhangelos Michael*, dating to the 13th cent. with icons and wall paintings of the 16th cent. According to tradition, the church was part of the former monastery of **Archangel Michael** which is now in ruins.

GOUDHI — A citrus centre to the left. Ancient tombs were found here.

CHRYSOCHOU / Comes from the Greek word meaning gold and it is believed that some gold mines were operating here in the past. The land is very fertile and under the Turks it served as a centre of local administration.

A general view of Ayii Anargyri *(courtesy Ayii Anargyri hotel).*

Route E-2 via Kathikas

After **STROUMBI** turn left and you reach **KATHIKAS.** Apart from its wine, it is famous for producing excellent **Sultanas, Sutzoukos** (a product of grape juice, sugar, flour, almonds — a kind of quince paste); **Palouze** (a product of grape juice, sugar, flour — a kind of blancmange sweet). Also **Trahanas** (an ingredient for soup — a product of wheat dried in the sun in cubes). Ancient tombs were discovered here.

ARODES (Pano = Upper — Kato = Lower). The name Arodes originated from the island of Rhodes and was the property of the Knights of St. John of Jerusalem (Hospitallers). Around the countryside even up to Peyia and Kathikas are traces of Tombs and according to the explorer Hoggarth who visited the area in 1887-88, *"sarcophaghi, pottery and glass of Roman origin were found"*. He also mentioned *"near Pano Orodhes (Arodhes) a mile and a half down the slope and two miles above Lipati site is a unique specimen of a pierced monolith of unknown origin and near the stone are remains of a building"*.

INIA — An interesting small village of 600 inh. **DHROUSIA** was originally settled by the Greek Arcadians. Recently a hotel Apartment was built here with panoramic views of the Polis bay and was the result of a co-operative effort by the earlier villagers who emigrated to foreign lands. For countryside lovers it is an ideal spot to stay for a few days or longer.

A turning to the right takes you to **KRITOU TERRA** and to the nearby sister village of TERRA. Here are strong traces of Roman settlements. It was the birthplace of the famous *Haji Georghakis Kornesios* who was the great Dragoman (interpreter) of Cyprus from 1779-1809 and obtained great influence with the Turkish authorities and with his wealth he helped the poor and sick.

Just over a mile to the northeast is the church of *Ayia Ekaterini* which can only be reached on foot. The large medieval church may be interesting to enthusiasts. It has three aisles and some frescoes but check in the village for the key.

Further down the road to Polis you pass, on the right, the shrine of *Ayios Yeoryios* built in the mouth of a cave probably of Byzantine times. At **PRODHROMI** a left turning will take you to **LATCHI** and **BATHS OF APHRODITE,** a right turning to POLIS.

Village of Kathicas (photo: Stephanos Theodorou).

General view of Goudhi village

A general view of Polis as seen from the road towards the Baths of Aphrodite.

A view of Chrysochou Bay as seen from the Tourist Pavilion at Aphrodite Baths.

Fishing boats resting inside the idylic harbour of Lachi. The fish here is always fresh.

Above Top: Beach near Baths of Aphrodite.
Above: A typical street at Polis with some old houses. Below: The fruit and vegetable market at Polis; this is usually open every morning.

Above: The pond where Aphrodite used to come for relaxation and bath in the crystal clear water running from the slopes. They say that those bathing in here, retain their youth forever, although the water is not that clean now and it is not advisable to enter into the pool. Below: General view of part of the coastline around the Baths of Aphrodite toward Fontana Amorosa.

In the area around the Baths of Aphrodite and near the sea, artifacts of a chalcolithic period were recently discovered. Previous travellers and explorers mentioned that near the spring, old ruins were discovered, believed to be those of the lost colony of the Athenian settlement of Akamandes. Along the coastline in the sea bed, a mass of Roman pottery was found.

Ayios Yeoryios Island

There is an interesting tradition regarding the Byzantine hero Dhighenis. While here with his love, the Queen Regena (see Petra tou Dhigeni —   ) they had a quarrel. Queen Regena left him and tried to get away in a boat. In his rage he took a great rock which he threw at the boat; the rock missed and split into 3 pieces, the largest formed an island that is Ayios Yeoryios.

POLIS

Silver coin of Marion — King Timochares (obverse)
— 5th Cent. B.C. *(Courtesy Director of Antiquities,*

Polis or **Polis tis Chrysochou** is an expanding agricultural and tourist centre with over 1700 inhabitants. There is a good hotel and self catering establishments. Between the town and the sea (about a mile away) is a well organised camping site — *see under accommodation.*

Bichrome crater from Goudhi, 6th Cent. B.C.
(Courtsey Director of Antiquities, Cyprus Museum)

It can be used as a centre for excursions either to Akamas or the areas of Pomos and Pyrgos or the inland countryside and mountains. Some of the old buildings of Polis are very interesting and efforts have been made to restore some of them. Most of the main Banks have branches here and there is also a fruit and vegetable market. The two small churches are of some interest but the new church, although modern, is large and predominantly Byzantine in style. During the middle ages Polis was an important agricultural centre and the Turkish landowners used to breed stallions and it was here that the famous Paphos pony was bred.

Close to Polis to the east, was the anc' ~ity of **MARION.** It was founded arou. 10th cent. BC by Athenian settlers and for a short time flourished and influenced the surrounding areas. During the wars for the possession of the island between the Ptolemy of Egypt and Antigonus of Syria and Asia Minor, the king of Egypt, Ptolemy Lagus, attacked the city which came under the influence of Antigonus and it was razed to the ground in 312 BC. Later in 285-247 BC. Ptolemy Philadelphus rebuilt the city and renamed it **ARSINOE,** but it never regained its power and influence.

Right: Attic lekythos — 6th Cent. B.C. Left: Funerary relief stele of Onasis — 5th Cent. B.C. Both from Marion *(Courtesy Director of Antiquities,*

During the Frankish period it was renamed **POLIS** and here the Orthodox Bishop of Paphos was exiled in 1222 AD.

There is nothing to be seen of the old Kingdom, all the buildings were destroyed and it was stated that seamen bringing timber to this area from Cilicia in Asia Minor, returned with stones of the ruined buildings. Around 1886 some 441 tombs were found. Further excavations were carried out in 1889, 1891 and 1929, most of the finds were taken abroad and those that remained in the island are exhibited at the museum of Paphos and the Cyprus Museum — Nicosia. The tombs were afterwards covered.

The new church of Polis

Polis is now expanding as a small picturesque town attracting many visitors. Most come from Paphos on a day visit, but many prefer to stay here or the nearby Lachi area for a few days or for the whole of their holiday, and they enjoy peace and quiet.

LACHI

Taking the road east of Polis and passing close to the beach and sea, one reaches a very picturesque fishing harbour, **LACHI**. The place is well-known for its fresh fish which one can eat in the tavernas around the protected harbour. The view of the small fishing boats is really nice. Overnight accommodation can be found here, or at Polis. There are sandy beaches close by for swimming, and the surrounding countryside with the low hills is worth exploring. The area around the small harbour is now expanding with some hotels and self-catering apartments, better beach facilities and numerous tavernas.

BATHS OF APHRODITE

Driving further away from Polis, close to the sea, the road twists and turns and comes to an end at The **Baths of Aphrodite.** Here there is a small tourist pavilion which serves food — including good fresh fish — and drinks. Below there is a small beach, mainly pebbles, but the water is crystal clear. The sea is ideal for underwater exploration and diving clubs often visit the area. Above, among the carrob trees, you may camp freely.

The main purpose of our trip is to visit the Baths of Aphrodite which are within walking distance from the tourist pavilion. The bathing place of Aphrodite is a semi-cave covered with vegetation. Water drips down from a spring at the top into a pool of water. If one bathes in the pool, eternal youth would be bestowed, but unfortunately one is not allowed to enter the water. The legend says that Aphrodite used to bath here at the cave because of the coolness of the spring

water after her wanderings in the forest. The legend also says that Aphrodite used to bring her young lovers here, away from the eyes of the people. The thick vegetation around the spring renders the place beautiful and idyllic.

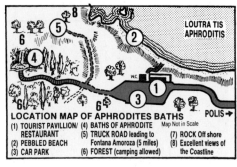

LOCATION MAP OF APHRODITES BATHS Map Not in Scale
(1) TOURIST PAVILLION/ (4) BATHS OF APHRODITE
    RESTAURANT   (5) TRUCK ROAD leading to   (7) ROCK Off shore
(2) PEBBLED BEACH   Fontana Amoroza (5 miles)   (8) Excellent views of
(3) CAR PARK   (6) FOREST (camping allowed)   the Coastline

Five miles further west, near the far end of the peninsula, is the Spring of Love — FONTANA AMOROSA. The area is uninhabited, but of extensive beauty, with one side being high mountains and the other rocky or sandy bays. If you are lucky enough to find the spot, you will see that there is nothing of importance here, but it is nevertheless worth visiting.

You will get a feeling of enormous joy just being in surroundings which so much inspired poets. The best way is to walk, since the road is not suitable for cars. It's about 5-6 miles walk. Alternatively, ask a fisherman at Lachi. For a small fee he may take you there.

A view of the beautiful little harbour of Lachi.

Above: Loutra tis Aphroditis beach, although not sandy provides crystal-clear waters and excellent underwater views for snogler divers. *Below:* Another view of the beautiful surrounding area.

Route F-1
to Pomos/Pyrgos

Although Pyrgos is under the Nicosia area, it is administered also from Paphos at present, because, since the Turkish occupation of the Lefka area, the coastal road has been cut off and is difficult to connect with Nicosia. The trip from Polis is long but exciting. However, you can drive as far as Pomos or Pakhyammos. The road which is very pleasant and in some places runs by the coast is under replanning and widening so this area will become more attractive to tourists.

MINOUSA — to the right of the road and before getting there, you go through **MAGOUNDA.** These are old mining areas which date back thousands of years. **LIMNI Mine** was the last to close and was operating until not so long ago.

ARGAGA is reached by another turning to the right along the main road. It is an agricultural centre with some 450 inh. The old church has been rebuilt recently. A truck road will take you inland into empty but beautiful countryside and to the old site of the monastery of *Ayios Merkourios* to the south east.

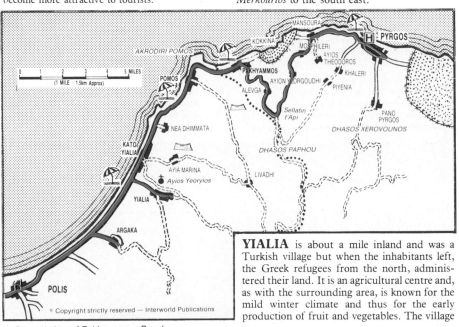

A General view of Pakhyammos Beach.

YIALIA is about a mile inland and was a Turkish village but when the inhabitants left, the Greek refugees from the north, administered their land. It is an agricultural centre and, as with the surrounding area, is known for the mild winter climate and thus for the early production of fruit and vegetables. The village

is built on the hills and the valley and provides beautiful views. Although a Frankish presence is in evidence, the church of *Ayios Cornuto* is of a rare shape.

KATO YIALIA (Lower Yialia).

Just to the northwest of Yialia and close to the beach. It is mainly a fishing village from people who came from **Ayia Marina,** inland to the east. There are some good beaches around here. The forest to the east of this area was largely burnt in 1974 by the Turkish invading forces, but as soon as the fires died, a programme of replanting started with great success.

POMOS

(some 500 inh.), a fishing centre but also becoming a tourist centre with a good beach and a couple of tavernas by the beach (summer only). Further to the north is *Pomos Point* where the coast is rocky but extremely lovely.

A truck road to the south east towards the Pomos Dam and down the gorge of the river *Livadhi* reveals beautiful scenery. Near the dams are the ruins of an old monastery but the church of *Khrysopateritissa* dated 16th cent.

survived and is of some interest because of its icons. A torturous journey will take you towards Stavros tis Psokas.

PAKHYAMMOS

a pretty settlement with a very nice beach. To the north is the Turkish occupied enclave of Kokkina and photography is not permitted here.

PYRGOS

is on the other side of the enclave and access is difficult as the coastal road cannot be used due to the objections of the Turkish occupied authorities. But a road has been made going around the enclave and then to Pyrgos. A trip to this area would be enjoyed mostly by nature lovers as there is not much else to be seen.

Sir Samuel Baker in his book "Cyprus as I saw it" wrote in 1879

"Pyrgos — This is one of the wildest parts of Cyprus. There is a village but the position is simply marked by the presence of one building above the sea-beach which has been a depot for the span and poles of pine . . ."

Above: General view of Pomos Cape. Below left: Small bay and fishing boats around the Pomos area
(photos: Stephanos Theodorou). Below right: 3 proud villagers from Lyso village.

Above: General view of Pyrgos, an ideal quiet place for those wishing to get away from civilization. *Below:* A view of the beautiful church of Panayia at Lyso.

LYSSOS FESTIVAL started in 1985 and has now become a major event where all the villagers come back to their roots as far as from Australia and South Africa. Other Paphians and tourists are most welcome to a weekend feast accompanied with music and dancing. Note: events take place in August and are well advertised with posters.

Route F-2 to Lyso

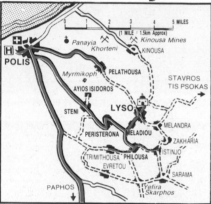

East of Polis is the village of **PETHALOUSA** situated south of **KINOUSA**. This area is the extension of the mines to the north as mentioned in route F-1. But it is believed that it was the living area of the miners as many rock cut and other tombs were found, also the remains of an old village. A block of stone with an inscription in Cypriotte writing was also found here. The church of *Panayia Khorteni* contains an old tomb and some frescoes.

From here a truck road will take you to **Lyso** to the southeast. However, for comfortable driving it is better to reach Lyso from the main road, turn left just outside Polis on the Polis-Paphos road. The countryside is beautiful.

STENI — a small agricultural village. To the northwest after the settlement of *Ayios Isidoros* is an area called **Myrmikoph** and the ruins of an old 13th cent. monastery of *Khrysolakouma*. It is believed that it was built on the site of an ancient temple. The monastery was abandoned in 1821 when its last abbot was hanged by the Turkish authorities.

PERISTERONA/MELADIOU small villages of no great importance.

LYSO about 500 inhabitants, but once a much larger village with over 1000 people, many emigrated abroad, mainly to Australia and Africa. The remaining are some of the most energetic people of Paphos and the village is listed as one of the cleanest and well kept from all the Cypriot villages. It is fascinating to wander around the beautiful village with the old houses and narrow streets. There is a nearly completed folk museum where objects of old domestic use will be exhibited, like the spinning wheels, the baking of bread etc. A small cafe is also planned behind the museum, in the court yard. But a visit to the Kafenion will provide you with refreshments.

The church of *Panayia Khryseleousa* is of medieval origin and a coat of arms of the Latin period is to be seen. Some parts of the church show a certain Gothic influence and there are some icons of interest. Below the church is the *Vrysi* (water fountain) with continuous running cool water. Once Lyso was famous for the amount of water which was available all the year round.

In the areas of Trimithousa, to Maladiou and here at Lyso, traces of old habitation and ancient tombs were found.

From here you may reach **Stavros tis Psokas** (but the road is difficult), or go south east and explore the area which provides beautiful scenery with views of high mountains, valleys, gorges, vineyards, carrob and almond trees and in some places citrus, but the driving is hard. It includes the villages of **MELOUNDA, ZUKHARIA,** The **Junction of Istinjo, PHILOUSA,** and **TRIMITHOUSA** which although of no great importance played some part in the islands' history during the Turkish occupation when a well-to-do Turk Giaour Imam, raged at the repressive measures against the peasants from the Turkish governor of Nicosia and in 1833 started a revolt which spread throughout Paphos and for many months he was in control of the district but in the end the revolution came to a tragic end.

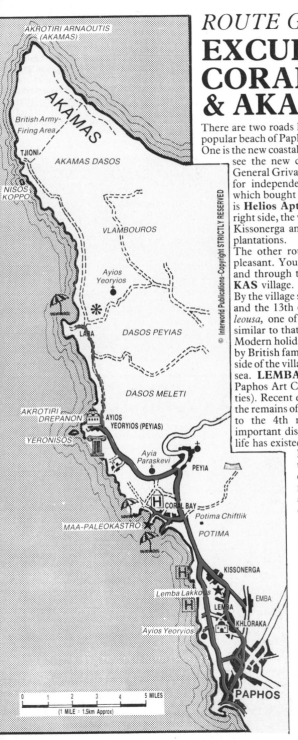

ROUTE G-
EXCURSION TO CORAL BAY & AKAMAS

There are two roads leading to Coral Bay — the most popular beach of Paphos and the largest tourist village. One is the new coastal road. Half way to the left you will see the new church of *Ayios Yeoryios* where General Grivas, leader of EOKA in the struggle for independence, landed in 1954. The boat which bought him is kept here. Then to the left is **Helios Apts** and **Cynthiana Hotel,** to the right side, the villages of Khlorakas, Lemba and Kissonerga and all are surrounded by banana plantations.

The other route is the old road which is as pleasant. You go through the town of Paphos and through the northern part of **KHLORA-KAS** village. Ancient tombs were found here. By the village square is the large modern church and the 13th cent. church of *Panayia Khryse-leousa,* one of the rarest of its type in Cyprus, similar to that of Ayios Theodosios at Adhelia. Modern holiday homes, some of them occupied by British families, have been built on the south side of the village with commanding views of the sea. **LEMBA** — A small village where the Paphos Art College operates (see under activities). Recent excavations have brought to light the remains of very early civilisations going back to the 4th millenium BC. This is a very important discovery giving clear evidence that life has existed in Paphos from that time.

KISSONERGA. Was built in the middle ages as an agricultural estate, although remains have been found of even earlier civilisations, a Byzantine watch tower and church is in ruins outside the village. It is a centre for banana plantations and to the south is Cynthiana hotel.

Between the village and Coral Bay, towards the northern side, close to the old bridge, is a site called *Potima* and in the middle ages Fossil remains of **Hippopotamus Minutus** were found. It is very interesting as fossils of this pigmy hippopotamus were found only in Cyprus, Malta and Crete. When the fossils were discovered the local people thought that they were remains of Christian Martyrs who were persecuted by the Romans and called the place *Ayii Planentes* (discovered Saints).

77

Archaeological sites of the area

LEMBA - LAKKOUS
to the south-western outskirts of Lemba village, a large chalcolithic site; the most important of the western coast of Paphos c. 3000-2500 BC. Circular houses have been discovered together with burial places and objects discovered include a beautiful necklace, rich variety of pottery, limestone female figurines and other items. The place is fenced.

KISSONERGA MOSPHILIA & MY-LOUTHKIA
to the north of Lemba and close to the outskirts of Kissonerga and near to Lemba-Lakkous. The first of the Chalcolithic period; finds include female terracotta figurines and red type pottery. The latter is of less importance dating to the end of the Neolithic beginning of Chalcolithic periods. Both places are fenced.

Above: Cape Drepanun ancient Basilica.
Left: Ancient site of Maa-Paleokastro.
(Courtesy Cyprus Museum)

CAPE DREPANUN
Originally a Roman town and harbour, the area of Ayios Yeoryios Peyias became an important place to the Christians during the 6th cent AD. Three basilicas were erected here. The main one was a 3 aisled church; excavations carried out show the extent of the buildings including a spacious baptistry, parts of corinthian columns and geometric mosaic floors. The area is fenced but you can observe it from the sides.
Caves which are cut into rock below the cliffs can be explored but be aware of falling rocks. There's still no sufficient information of their actual use.

MAA - PALEOKASTRO
Situated at the edge of the peninsula between the Coral and Corallia Bays, served as a military outspot for the Greek settlers (c. 1230-1200 BC) who were arriving in those years in great numbers. Its defensive character is shown by the remains of Cyclopean Walls to the northern part of the settlement. The site is fenced.

CORAL BAY

This lovely area is developing as a tourist attraction and holiday village, with houses owned by locals as well as many British, who have established a small but well organised community. There are several tavernas here where one can simply order drinks, or have a good freshly-cooked meal. The sandy beaches are clean and ideal for children and non-swimmers, since the water is very shallow and therefore very safe. Sea sports facilities are available in these very popular beaches of Paphos.

At the far end and between the two major bays, on a peninsular just beyond the taverna, stand the ruins of **Maa-Paleokastro,** an early Bronze Age settlement which was fortified. It is also believed that the area was a major desembarkation point of the new settlers arriving from Greece. The area has been fenced off since excavation work is continuing, although visitors may enter if work is in progress and the gates open. Huge stones, which were part of the fortification, are still visible.

Coming back onto the main road and turning left we reach the picturesque village of **PEYIA,** which has a lovely church and

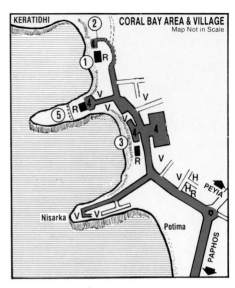

(1) **CORALLIA BAY/BEACH**
   & Windsurfing Facilities
(2) **CAMPING AREA (No Facilities)**
(3) **CORAL BAY/MAIN BEACH**
(4) **PARKING SPACES**
(5) **MAA-PALEOKASTRO**
   (ANCIENT SITE)

(R) **RESTAURANT**
(H) **HOTEL**
(V) **VILLAS-HOUSES**
(Please Note: Some new Accommodation is planned for the future)

A view of Coral Bay, the Golden Beach of Paphos. If you don't like lots of people, avoid July and August.

Coral Bay Beach — The most popular beach in the Paphos district.

Above: Two views from the Akamas area.
Below: Coral Bay in the Autumn.

The Keratidhi (Corallia) Beach, next to Coral Bay. The taverna here provides changing cabins and showers. A well organised wind-surfing school operates here and provides water sport facilities.

A view from the Taverna at Ayios Yeoryios with the Bay and the Yeronissos Island.

Sunset at Coral bay with Maa-Paleokastron Peninsula in the background.

An empty beach in the Lara area. The area is also a breeding place for turtles.

The mystery column at Tjioni

The Basilica at Ayios Yeoryios

The Coral Bay popular Beach and the Tourist village.

some interesting little houses which are very well kept. The village is of Byzantine origin. The view of the coastline from the Church is wonderful. South of the road after leaving Peyia there is a modern church, built on the site of an old monastery, which stopped functioning in 1788 AD. The church of Ayia Paraskevi is dedicated to Panayia tou Zalajon, the curer of varicose veins.

AYIOS YEORYIOS

Going through banana plantations one reaches a small settlement dominated by the small church of **Ayios Yeoryios.**

There is a taverna and a guest house where one can stay when exploring the surrounding area and there is a good beach for swimming below the village. From the top of the hill one can see a view of the small bay, which was used by the Romans for swimming and fishing. Fishing boats can be seen, adding extra attraction. The small island of Ayios Yeoryios (600 feet long and 60 feet wide) can be seen about 500 feet off-shore. On the island are the remains of what is thought to be a Neolithic settlement. Close to the settlement of

Mosaic Floor of the Basilica and the church of Ayios Yeoryios.

The tower of the church at Peyia village.

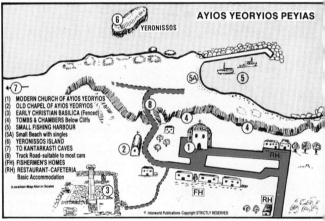

Ayios Yeoryios are early Christian churches and houses. Floor remains and mosaics and the main Basilica is open to the public during working hours and worth visiting. Below the cliff and above the fishing harbour and the beach, caves have been cleared and are open to the public. Burial Chambers were carved in the rock.

KANTARKASTOI

These are sea caves which can be reached either by sea or land. By land you may go there by descending a narrow path from the church of Ayios Yeoryios. The caves are about half a mile from the church to the

East. You can take the path which goes near the sea and after walking for three-quarters of an hour you will reach them. These are the only good sea caves to be seen in Cyprus. The caves are not all together and you have to walk from one place to another to see them all. Some of the caves are deep and the sea enters. Some of them communicate, the water entering one and coming out of another. The colours of the inside of the caves are wonderful — green and violet changing in the light which reflects from the water. The legend of these caves is that at the time of the Saracen raids the people of the village of Peyia ran to the mountains and forests in

Two views of Ayios Yeoryios Peyias area. *Above:* The dominating church of Ayios Yeoryios Peyias as viewed from the old Basilica. *Below:* The small but interesting small fishing harbour, a base of local fishermen. For a small fee they can take you around for a trip.

order to save their lives. Once they returned to the sea they saw many rocks in a row on the shore front. Then they realised that Ayios Yeoryios had protected them from the Saracens (Arabs) by throwing these rocks at the invaders. For better exploration you may ask a local fisherman from Ayios Yeoryios to take you there by boat for a small fee.

LARA

For the most adventurous a trip to Lara will provide empty sandy beaches for swimming, away from the crowds. However, to get there on the narrow twisting roads you need a good car. Do not drive after heavy rain (this applies mainly to winter visitors) as you may stick in mud. Also be aware of British army trucks which use the road on the way to Akamas for exercises. The road is not surfaced and full of stones some big.

Lara offers exotic surroundings and we believe that a small kafenion (cafeteria) is now operating. The area is also well-known for its turtle breeding.

DEEP INTO AKAMAS PENINSULA

Driving further away the road becomes more stoney but the forest of Akamas is beautiful. The beaches below are inviting and some of the coast is rocky with small islands — the largest being Koppo Island, which is interesting for its shape. The truck road ends at a small bay called **TJIONI**. The area around here is unfortunately closed when the British army practices, but this does not often happen.

The fascinating aspect of this place is a weather-beaten column which sticks out of the water and is believed to be a mooring column. The ruins of a pier (mainly rock now) can be seen nearby. The Romans had a port here and one wonders if the lost city of Akamas (named after the Athenian Akamanthus who founded it after the Trojan War) is either buried nearby or submerged under water. Archaeologists are still looking for the lost Royal city.

In this area, beware of unexploded shells.

Climbing up the mountain from here is a very poor truck route which one could attempt **with a Landrover only.** On the top of the mountains you can see the remains of British anti-aircraft installations from the Second World War. The forest is superb and the surrounding views wonderful. The truck road will take you over the other side of the mountains to the Fontana Amoroza area and then to Baths of Aphrodite Lachi and Polis.

One of the isolated beaches of Lara, which one can reach by a very strong car or a landrover. During the summer there are boat trips from Paphos harbour an ideal way to reach this place for a swim, exploration and a barbeque.

AKAMAS — Summary

This area is mysterious, not only to foreign visitors but also to locals. It is only visited by fishermen, hunters, the British army for exercises and some adventurous tourists. It is more or less in its natural state. However, this will change soon, as a coastal road is planned all the way up the Baths of Aphrodite and tourist establishments will be erected, although there is now a growing opposition which prefers the area to remain in its natural state and declared a National Park. You can help by expressing your views, so if you are a lover of nature, explore it now, as Hoggarth did in 1887-88 who wrote:

> **"It is a sterile corner of Cyprus, thickly covered with scrub, abounding in deep gullies and bold rock formations, the central spine being broken into bold peaks or miniature table mountains; here and there in a tiny valley is a cultivated patch, but nine tenths of the district produces nothing but game . . ."**

Although the area is now uninhabited, there are many signs that this was not always so. At the headland of Cape Drepano by Ayios Yeoryios, Roman and Byzantine settlements were discovered; inland, signs of ruined Byzantine churches in the forest of Meleti, together with rock cut tombs of unknown origin and further up at Lara and the area of Konon there is an abandoned, ancient settlement. This and the church of Ayios Konon can be seen just under 1 mile inland among he pines. The bay of Tjioni used to be a Roman settlement most submerged under water.

ROUTE H
The Valley of Dhiarizos

This is an area worth exploring and it will take more or less a day to complete. Refreshments can be bought from the Kafenion in any of the villages along the route, although food may not be that easy to find. A packed lunch would do nicely.

Along the main Paphos — Limassol road you turn left before Kouklia, towards the newly built Aspro-kremmos Dam (Stavrokonos) — one of the largest in Cyprus which you can observe from the top. At the road junction you follow the sign for Nikoklia (should you decide to take the left turning, you go up the route the other way round).

NIKOKLIA

An ancient settlement attached to Kouklia (to the east) and given the name of the last king of Paphos Nikokles — 320 BC. The modern village is scenic and situated by the west bank of the river. The old church has several interesting icons.

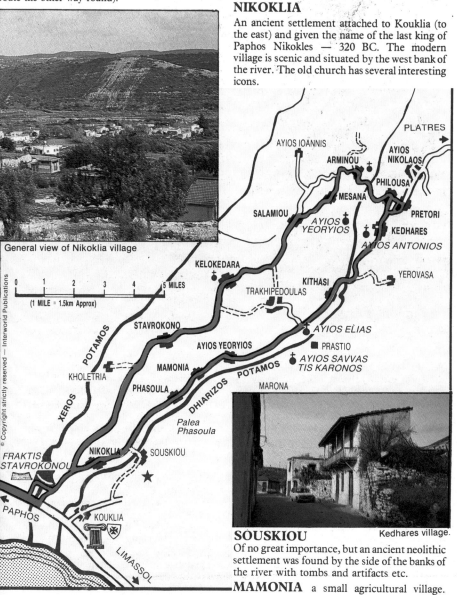

General view of Nikoklia village

Kedhares village.

SOUSKIOU

Of no great importance, but an ancient neolithic settlement was found by the side of the banks of the river with tombs and artifacts etc.

MAMONIA a small agricultural village.

85

Souskiou village and the valley of Dhiarizos river

The Dhiarizos river and valley (during the summer is dry).

The Church of Salamiou village.

The famous Paphos donkey, to be seen in all the villages.

AYIOS YEORYIOS — small village. On the north east, by the west side of the river is an old rock cut tomb with the chapel of *Ayios Elias* built by its side. Over the other side of the river is the abandoned settlement of **Prastio** and a late 15th century chapel, now deserted.

Just under a mile south west of Prastio are the remains of a once prosperous monastery, that of

---

SOUSKIOU-VATHYRKAKAS

situated between Kouklia 2km to the northeast and Souskiou village 1.5km to the southwest. An important Chalcolithic settlement. Finds include pendants, female figurines and the largest statuette found in Cyprus of that period, illegally exported and now in private hands in Europe. The area is fenced. Tombs of other periods were discovered close by.

Ayios Savvas tis Karonos. This isolated monastery is of unknown origin but it is believed it was established in the 12th-13th cent. An inscription written in 1501 on the west door reads:

> "It must be that a king first built this monastery, which time has so damaged. May God on the awful day of Judgement remember the Evarch of this monastery who in 1501 repaired and beautified this church".

The existing church has some interesting icons and is in good condition. Both the church and some buildings show Gothic influence and have good carved stone work.

In 1568 a fire destroyed the monastery. According to Abbot Gerasimus who sent a letter to king James II, it was struck by lightning and all the monastery, except the church, was destroyed. The king agreed to have it rebuilt on condition that a mass was said for ever for his soul.

Some of the buildings are now used by farmers. The only way to reach this place is by foot.

After **KITHASI** the road starts climbing upwards and the view of the river and the valley is really beautiful. To the left is the restored church of *Ayios Antonios*.

KEDHARES. A picturesque small village.

PRETORI — The church has an interesting 16th cent. icon of the Virgin. It is believed that the name Pretori was given from a Roman general called Prator who had a summer villa here.

From here, if you follow the road that twists up north, you go to Platres through the village of **Ayios Nicolaos.** Up to 1928 the 13th century church in the village had two altars, one Latin and one Orthodox.

Turning towards the west and down the valley through **PHILOUSA** and then up the other side you reach **ARMINOU.** Armenians used to live here who came to Cyprus as refugees. The church of *Stavros* is 18th century.

AYIOS IOANNIS situated to the north of the main road. This was a Turkish village but the inhabitants went to the north of Cyprus and most of the houses are now empty. To the north is the truck road leading to the Bridge of Roudhias

MESANA — A small village with vineyards. Down in the river valley by the south east of the village is the isolated church of *Ayios Yeoryios* where there used to be a monastery. There are some interesting icons.

SALAMIOU — A big village with a large impressive church. The village, like all the others of the area, produces some grapes but mainly almonds, carrobs and sheep.

KELOGEDARA

A picturesque village with scenic views of the valley to the west of the river Xeros Potamos where the remains of the 14th-15th cent. monastery of *Santi* can be seen. The church of *Panayia Eleousa* is famous for its hexagonal dome.

After driving through the village of *STAVRO-GONNOU* you eventually reach the junction from where you went to Nikoklia, back to the main road and to Paphos.

General view of a geologically interesting countryside near the village of Kedhares.

ROUTE I
TO PISSOURI BAY

Although Pissouri is within the Limassol district, it is within the Paphos postal administration. A visit to the Bay can be enjoyed by everyone, as it offers good swimming and excellent eating.

Take the main road from Paphos to Limassol, pass Kouklia and the Birthplace of Aphrodite (Petra tou Romiou) and climb upwards and inland. Then you reach Pissouri. This is not the actual village which is ½ mile to the east on the side to the mountain. The cafes here were established many years ago as a stopping place when the road was very narrow and twisting and a journey would have taken three times as long as now.

Continuing along the main road down the valley on a straight stretch of the road you will see the signs for the Pissouri Beach Hotel to the right. Here you drive through one of the best vineyards of Cyprus which produces **Sultani Table Grapes.** Eventually you reach the Bay which is now a major tourist centre with apartments and the impressive Pissouri Beach hotel that has a large swimming pool and a good restaurant which caters for non-residents There are also tavernas in the summer where you can enjoy Cypriot cooking. At the hotel, changing cabins and showers are available for a small charge.

The beach is long and provides good swimming except in some places where pebbles make it a little uncomfortable.

Driving time about 45 minutes.

Pissouri Beach

CHAPTER 4
USEFUL THINGS TO KNOW

Please note that some of the details quoted below and in previous pages change from time to time, therefore to be really sure that the information you have is correct and up to date you are advised to visit the:

> **Tourist Information Office**
> **3 Gladstone Street, Paphos**
> **Tel 232841**

Cyprus Head Office:
18 Th. Theodotou Street, P.O. Box 4535, Nicosia
Tel: (02) 443374

United Kingdom Office:
213 Regent Street, London W1R 8DA
Tel: 01-734 9822

TRAVELLING AROUND

If you have arranged an all inclusive tour, transfers from the airport to your hotel and vise a versa are arranged. However, there are regular taxi services which are very reasonably priced. Bus services also exist with connections to all towns and the airport.

TAXIS
Shared taxi services run frequently from town to town for a fixed price and most of them will take you to your destination address. Night services between towns are infrequent if they exist at all, so make sure to check for their last run.

The Paphos to Limassol journey is still under CY£2.00. To travel around Paphos itself and the surrounding countryside, a taxi will be happy to take you anywhere at any time. The receptionist at your establishment will be happy to arrange a taxi for you. The main taxi services include: KARYDAS (tel 32459), KYPROS (tel 32376) KYRIAKOS (tel 33181), MAKRIS (tel 32538).

BUSES
Bus services connect Paphos with the other towns, they take longer for the journey although they charge less. They are operated by **KEMEK Bus Company, Paphos office tel 32272.**

There is also a well organised bus service run by ALEPA Ltd which travels within the town, the harbour, the hotels and the ancient ruins and monuments between 6am-5pm daily (Sat. & Sun. 9am-5pm). Buses run every 30 minutes. There is also a regular

service, mainly in the summer to Coral Bay beach starting from Pervola bus station. The same company also runs services to various villages and tourist places such as Kouklia, Polis, Panayia, Pomos etc. For up to date time-tables telephone 34252 or 34410.

COACH TOURS
Sightseeing tours can be arranged by tourist agencies to visit important places in Paphos and further afield. They include Louis Tourist Agency, Aeolos Travel, Paradise Island Travel, Blue Sea Travel, Geko Tours, Salamis Tours.

CAR HIRE
If you do not have car-hire included in your all inclusive tour, you may hire a car in Paphos — any type of car for any period of time. However, one must remember there may be difficulties in hiring a car immediately in the busy months of July and August and prior arrangements are recommended. Please also check what an insurance policy covers. The main car hire firms are: PETSAS (tel 35522); EUROPCAR (tel 34149); GECO TOURS (tel 32347); HERTZ (tel 33985); LOUIS TOURIST (tel 33320); KLEOPAS (tel 32508); SECURITY TRAVEL (tel 33278); BUDGET (tel 35100).

BIKES & MOTORBIKES
This is an easy way to travel around especially for short distances and you can hire bikes or motorbikes from hotels or various

tourist shops which specialise. Places for hiring also exist at Polis and Lachi.

Distances from Paphos Town to: in miles.

Peyia	10
Ayios Yeoryios	17
Tsada	7
Kathikas	16
Polis	25
Pomos	37
Lyso	31
Stroumbi	12
Phiti	20
Panayia	25
Galataria	24
Pendalia	22
Konia	2½
Episkopi	9½
Timi	6
Kedhares	25
Pretori	26
Kouklia	10
Ayios Neophitos	6
Petra tou Romiou	15
Stavros tis Psokas	32
Aphrodites Baths	30
Khrysorroyiatissa	27
Coral Bay	7
Paphos Airport	8
Larnaca Airport	91
Limassol	44
Larnaca	89
Platres	39
Nicosia	97

PLEASE REMEMBER

a) In Cyprus you drive on the same side of the road as in Britain.

b) Petrol stations close Sat. afternoon, Sunday all day and Holidays.

c) Parking meters exist in some parts of the town.

d) Always, please take. care of pedestrians, cyclists, and bad drivers. — Drive within the limits.

ACTIVITIES

SEA ACTIVITIES for swimming and beaches — see pages 82-83.

WATERSPORTS: Watersports are now very popular in Paphos and can be enjoyed mainly in the beaches of Coral and Corailia Bays, by the harbour and at major hotels such as the Paphos Beach, Cypria Maris, Cynthiana and Pissouri Beach and include windsurfing, boating, limited sailing, waterskiing, fishing expeditions. Cypria Maris provides an indoor pool and a gym. At Corallia Bay, there is a well organised windsurfing school with qualified instructors open to beginners and more advanced surfers.

FISHING EXPEDITIONS: Some fishing can be done inland in reservoirs after obtaining a permit from the fisheries department. Fishing in the sea along the coast is without restrictions. Some hotels organise individual or small party expeditions around Coral Bay, Lara, Akamas, Lachi, You may approach some fishermen in Paphos and Lachi harbour who for a fee may take you fishing.

SEA CRUISES: There is a limited summer service to isolated or popular beaches operating from the harbour and provide drinks and lunch. Information can be obtained from the harbour or your hotel.

UNDERWATER EXPLORATION: Paphos, over the last few years has become a centre for professional and amateur divers from all over Western Europe. The excellent climate of Paphos, the facilities of the harbour, the hard work of local people and professional British divers who are now residents of Paphos, have contributed to this popular expansion. The **CYDIVE** centre is situated close to the harbour and has its own premises at Posidonos Avenue — Kato Paphos — Tel. (061) 34271 and is run by Mr. Phivos Roussis from whom any information can be obtained. The club is called **DIVERS DEN** where divers and friends meet for a drink or a chat also for slide shows, barbeques or to plan their next excursion. CYDIVE is organised to a high degree of proficiency and has highly qualified and expert instructors who will undertake to supervise other divers. They have internationally accepted qualifications such as the BS-AC and ASA. They also teach groups and individuals. The club is very well equipped with suites and all necessary equipment, boats and landrovers. Any visitor to Paphos can enjoy the shores and coast which provide excellent marine life, some old and new wrecks, signs of submerged ruins, caves and valleys. Underwater photography shows an abundance of colourful marine life with subjects such as octopus, moray, eels, large groupers, soldier fish, sponges, gorgonians sea shells etc.

Above: A group of Cy-dive divers exploring the depths of the Paphian sea.
Left: A Cy-dive diver explores a sea wreck.
(Courtesy Cy-dive)

Above: Corallia Bay — Windsurfing has become a popular sport all along the Paphian coast.
Left Top: Coral Bay — Beaches, even when crowded are ideal places for basic sporting activities.
Left: A group of divers during their first lessons.

OTHER ACTIVITIES – For such activities you can contact the Tourism Information Office at Paphos.

TENNIS: Some hotels provide tennis facilities, mainly for residents. There is a tennis court in the public gardens near the 28th October Square which is open to all.

HUNTING: This is very popular in Cyprus and Paphos mountains provide excellent hunting places. Hunting is permitted in special areas only and at certain periods and a special licence is required.

PHOTOGRAPHY: Paphos is an ideal place for landscape photography. Local photographic shops provide all well known films and can also develop and print within 24 hours. Photography, however, as in all other countries is prohibited in areas near military camps and around Pachiammos and Pyrgos close to areas occupied by the Turkish army.

HORSE RIDING: A riding centre operates in Paphos and tuition is available to beginners and experienced riders. Further details from Paphos Riding Centre Tel. 33966 or 34508 (evening) P.O. Box 302 — Paphos.

SPORTS: Paphos has two football teams; and nearly all matches attract good crowds.
In athletics you can train or participate with local athletes. There are two stadiums with limited athletic facilities.

SOCIETIES: Two International societies, LYONS and ROTARY clubs have branches in Paphos and regular meetings take place at the Paphos Beach Hotel.

PAPHOS ART COLLEGE: Established in 1978 it is situated in the village of Lemba by the side of a hill overlooking the sea and is run by Stass Paraskos who at present is a senior lecturer at Canterbury College of Art. It is an advanced school mainly for postgraduate students, operates through the year and has special tuition classes during the summer.
This is ideal for artists wishing to paint in the open air. The clear colours and light and the beautiful landscapes provide the artist with some unbeatable imagination for his work.

91

THE BEACHES OF PAPHOS

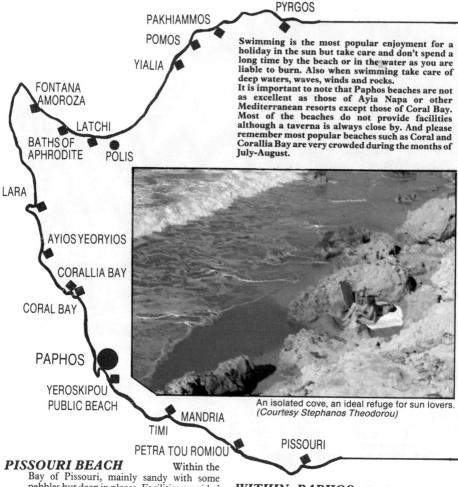

PYRGOS

PAKHIAMMOS

POMOS

YIALIA

FONTANA AMOROZA

LATCHI

BATHS OF APHRODITE

POLIS

LARA

AYIOS YEORYIOS

CORALLIA BAY

CORAL BAY

PAPHOS

YEROSKIPOU PUBLIC BEACH

MANDRIA

TIMI

PETRA TOU ROMIOU

PISSOURI

Swimming is the most popular enjoyment for a holiday in the sun but take care and don't spend a long time by the beach or in the water as you are liable to burn. Also when swimming take care of deep waters, waves, winds and rocks.

It is important to note that Paphos beaches are not as excellent as those of Ayia Napa or other Mediterranean resorts except those of Coral Bay. Most of the beaches do not provide facilities although a taverna is always close by. And please remember most popular beaches such as Coral and Corallia Bay are very crowded during the months of July-August.

An isolated cove, an ideal refuge for sun lovers. *(Courtesy Stephanos Theodorou)*

PISSOURI BEACH
Within the Bay of Pissouri, mainly sandy with some pebbles but deep in places. Facilities provided by the hotel and tavernas.

PETRA TOU ROMIOU
Aphrodites Birthplace — Park carefully here. Mainly sandy bays with pebbles and some rocks. Be careful of deep areas and undercurrents. The tourist pavilion a short distance up the hill is ideal for a meal afterwards.

MANDRIA:
A partly sandy beach which is open to southern winds.

TIMI:
Two beaches, one partly sandy with a taverna-restaurant and a place for camping.

YEROSKIPOU PUBLIC BEACH:
To the east of Paphos, with changing cabins and showers, restaurant-cafeteria-grass lawn. The beach is a mixture of sand, shingles and sea weeds. Many sea sports are available.

WITHIN PAPHOS:
Small stretches of beach, most popular in front of Paphos Beach hotel and another to the east. Also near the lighthouse. Public baths to the west of Annabelle are ideal for diving; changing rooms and showers. Do not expect long beaches in the Paphos town area as most of the coast is rocky and in places polluted

CORAL BAY
The most popular during the summer, however empty in early morning and late afternoon. Nice sand and shallow waters. Cafes-restaurants and facilities.

CORALLIA BAY:
Next to Coral Bay, good sandy beach, but can change after a heavy winter. Centre of windsurfing and other sports. Restaurant, shop, showers.

AYIOS YEORYIOS
More of an idylic little harbour than a beach, but can provide some bathing. Cafeterias and restaurant.

LARA (page 88): Excellent sandy beaches mainly empty due to bad road connections ideal for adventurers.

FONTANA AMOROZA: Isolated coastline of unique beauty with small coves with sand and pebbles; difficult to reach.

BATHS OF APHRODITE
Mainly pebble but with some sand, excellent clear waters, small coves and good rock formations. The tourist pavilion offers changing and shower facilities and excellent fish.

LATCHI AREA
Long stretches of sandy beaches with some pebbles at places to the east and west of the harbour. Numerous tavernas provide meals and refreshments.

POLIS: Long beaches along the town which are 1-2 miles inland. The best way to reach the beach is through the camping site.

YIALIA AREA
Main road runs along the beach (separated at places with houses). However, the long beaches are mainly pebbled and not always clean.

POMOS-PAKHYAMMOS
At places are some small sheltered bays with empty beaches. At Pakhyammos the beach is long and mainly sandy and empty.

PYRGOS
Just before entering the village. An excellent beach with a taverna and showers.

Within the village by the hotel Tolon, a long pebbled beach; restaurants and tavernas.

An ideal spot for the townsfolk to relax.

Above: The Beach at TIMI — *Right:* One of the beaches near the Latchi area.
Below: The Yeroskipou public Beach which provides all the facilities.

ENTERTAINMENT — EATING OUT

Since Paphos became a major tourist centre, various pubs, tavernas and other places of entertainment have mushroomed, mainly in Kato Paphos, close to the hotels and the harbour. It is difficult for us to mention the names of the various establishments or express our opinion regarding the service or cuisine, however, by studying advertisements or asking around you will get some idea as to what suits you.

NIGHT CLUBS/BOUZOUKIA

These places provide Greek music and singing, mainly live and you can participate in the singing and dancing. They are mainly open from about 11pm up to the early hours and they serve mainly drinks. There are a number of them in Paphos. You may also find during the summer a cabaret night club where various shows take place and where food is served. If in doubt, check with your hotel personnel, they will be glad to advise you where to go.

Some of the **tavernas** which provide eating may also have occassional evenings of bouzouki music, singing and folk dancing during the summer.

HOTEL ENTERTAINMENT

During the tourist season, the hotels and some of the apartments have various evening functions such as beach parties, or night of Greek Cypriot folk dancing, singing and eating and some, like the Paphos Beach provide further events such as Miss Aphrodite contest, wine tasting , etc. You are free to go around the various hotels and check the programmes and attend their functions. You may even attend one of the many annual Balls given by various clubs and organisations of Paphos (dinner and dance) which occur throughout the year mainly in hotels.

DINING & DRINKING

Eating out, whether you have made full board or half board arrangements with your hotel, is a must, not only for tasting the delicious local specialities but also to enjoy the atmosphere and taste the various wines of Cyprus which include:

White Wines:
Keo Hock, Aphrodite, Fair Lady, White Lady, Bellapais, Arsinoe, St. Panteleimon, Demi-sec, Thisbe, Graves.
Red Wines:
Othello, Afames, Dark Lady, Mermes, Keo Claret, Olympus Claret, Dommain, D'Athera.
Rose:
Rosella, Rose, Etko, Rosita, Rose Sodap.
Sweet:
Muscat, Malaga, Commandaria Port.
Cyprus Sherry:
Keo Fino, Keo Cream, Pale dry, Emva Cream, Olympus dry, Olympus Medium, Kyp.

Cyprus Brandy is cheap and tasty. There are various brands some stronger than others, so ask the waiter for advice. Brandy Sour is recommended.

Apart from the Hotels and Apartments which have their own restaurant and welcome visitors, you can enjoy a nice Cypriot meal at the various Tavernas, Kebab Houses and Fish Restaurants which are all over the town and the harbour. Most of them offer local decor and Greek atmosphere and in the summer you eat outside in the fresh air. Most meals are Cypriot but if you prefer steaks or simple food like an omelette, do not hesitate to ask even if it isn't on the menu. They will be very pleased to provide you with a meal to your own taste.

Cafeterias and Bars

These provide refreshments, coffee, drinks and beers but also provide some meals and serve sandwiches, ice cream and cakes. Many of them have their chairs and tables on a wide pavement by the road and you can sit there as long as you wish to watch the world go by

Pubs

These mainly try to promote the British pub atmosphere. They are pleasant to visit and there are no restrictions to their opening hours, some can go up to 2am. You will find all local and International drinks including many whisky brands, gin and probably a wider selection of beers than the two lager brands which are the only ones served in the island.

For your eating you may try the MEZE. This is a collection of either fish or meat appetizers including cheeses, salads and dips and are selected from the various dishes which we describe below and some can also be served as individual meals.

PORK SPECIALITIES

Souvlakia (kebabs) — small pieces of meat on skewer, cooked over charcoal. Instead of pork, lamb can also be used.

Afelia— marinated pork with wine and herbs.

Sheftalia — minced meat (marinated) whipped as a sausage and cooked on charcoal.

Zalatina — Braun (pork cooked in broth with meat and bitter orange & lemon).

Loukanika — spicy meat sausages, fried or grilled.

Lounza — smoked pork fillets, marinated and served grilled or fried.

94

Above and Below: Scenes of CYPRIOT NIGHT entertainment. This is a regular event, at least once weekly in most hotels and other large establishments, not only for the resident guests but also for everyone. These nights apart from the traditional dancing and music, also provide an excellent cuisine which is either meze of buffet.

Hiromeri — leg of pork marinated in wine and smoked, served in slices.

Kolokasi — Jerusalem artichoke cooked with pork.

OTHER MEAT & MINCED SPECIALITIES

Kleftiko — Lamb meat cooked slowly in the oven.

Souvla — Large pieces of Lamb cooked slowly over charcoal. This is really delicious when nicely cooked.

Kieftedes — small fried minced meatballs.

Mousaka — layers of potatoes, aubergines and mince meat covered with bechamel cream and baked in oven.

Stiphado / Beef casserole, with small onions, red wine etc.

Tava — Lamb or Beef casserole, cooked in small pots.

Koupepia — Stuffed vine leaves with minced meat, tomato & lemon sauce.

Dolmadhes (Yemista) — Stuffed vegetables (tomatoes, aubergines, peppers or courgettes) with minced meat, rice and herbs.

Koupes — made of crushed wheat "rolls" filled with minced meat, onion, parsley and cinnamon, and fried.

SOUPS

Yuvarlakia Avgolemono / minced meat balls in egg and lemon broth.

Argolemono — chicken pieces or chicken stock in egg and lemon broth and rice.

Trahana — A wheat and sour milk soup.

Patsha — Lamb's brain and tongue or head soup.

PASTA

Yiuvetsi — Pilaf with barley-like macaroni and meat.

Ravioles — made with cheese filling.

Pasticcio (Makaroni tou fournou) — baked macaroni with minced meat filling and bechamel sauce.

DIPS

Taramosalata — smoked cod's roe puree.

Tahini — Sesame meal creamy puree.

Talatouri — cucumber and yoghurt with crushed garlic.

Houmous — chick peas puree.

CHEESES

Fetta — white cheese with sharp, salty paste usually mixed with salad.

Halloumi — white cheese made from goat's milk, the most popular cheese in Cyprus.

FISH DISHES

Barbounia — Red mullet. A tasty fish but with small bones.

Xyphias — Swordfish. Very tasty, usually grilled.

Maridhes — Whitebait.

Kalamaria — Squid, cut in rings or small pieces and fried.

Octapodi — Octupus either cooked as a stew, with red wine or served cold with lemon sauce.

In a good Cypriot taverna or restaurant you are always welcome to go into the kitchen and discuss what you wish to eat and if you wish to enjoy a fish meal, you may be shown a selection from which you can choose your own.

RESSI (Wheat Pilaf)

Once considered as the National Cypriot food, is served in many functions and village festivals, some villages organised their special RESSI FESTIVAL. Ingredients include wheat, lamb's meat, and the tail. Chicken meat can also be added. It takes 5-6 hours to prepare. It is so popular in Paphos and the locals always say "A wedding without Ressi is like winter without rain".

Enjoying the Cyprus cooking in a taverna by the Paphos harbour (courtesy, Cyprus Tourism Organisation).

SHOPPING

Shopping is part of every visitor's holiday enjoyment, and Paphos, like every other tourist centre, provides a large selection of items to suit everyone. However be careful of cheap imitations which are produced in some Asian countries. Although most of the shops are Europeanised in both looks and attitudes and their prices are displayed, you may care to try the old eastern tradition of bargaining.

Most of the shopkeepers are owners thus providing a friendly and very personal service, some may even offer you coffee or a drink. Most of them speak English.

Whether you shop for souvenirs, or you want clothes, toiletries, you will find that most of the items are available. Good handicraft, pottery and jewellery are ideal items to purchase, but search for the good shops.

Food. For fresh fruit, vegetables, meat and fish, visit the Paphos public market   Other shops are around the town and close to most hotels and in Polis. They will supply the vegetables, fruit and food provisions mainly needed by those in self catering accommodation. If you are confused with the weight OKA (or OKE), 1 OKA + 400 drams (144 drams + 1lb). So it is just 2¾ lbs. Now the official weight has become the KILO.

When you do shopping, do it in a leisurely way. It is best to go either in the early morning or late afternoon when it is cooler.

Further confusion may occur with the currency as although the official currency is C£1 = 100 cents, most of the locals calculate prices to the old "shillings" when £1 = 20 shillings, so try not to get confused.

Shopping hours vary, but due to midday siesta most of the shops open between 8am-1pm and 4pm-7pm (in winter there is a shorter lunch break and they close earlier at night). Saturday is a half day. In some tourist areas shops are open longer hours.

Above Top: Sponges can be bought in Paphos at less than ⅓ the price you will pay at home. *Above:* A travelling toy shop. These travelling merchants were the heart and soul of every village event, being continually on the move and selling their merchandise including clothes, toys, china, food products. Few remain now but still give colour to the square of the village for a few days. *Below:* The famous Paphos woven material with cross-stitched patterns. Most popular are the **PHITIOTICA** including lace of excellent quality.

FESTIVALS

There are a number of popular festivals which attract interest and create fun for all the family. There are also some less important local activities and festivals which are not mentioned here. If you are interested, watch out for local advertising.

The major festivals are:

PAPHOS CARNIVAL

This is something new to Paphos and it started in 1983 as a continuation of a very old tradition and in competition to the even larger carnival of Limassol. One of the masterminds of this event is the very progressive and well liked mayor of Paphos Mr. Agrotis. The carnival takes place during the weekend preceding Lent, with processions of floats, bands the singing of songs, dancing etc. During the week children dress in various fancy costumes and visit their friends to see if they can be recognised. Local organisations give dances.

ANTHESTIRIA

This is a flower festival, and has been well established in Paphos for many years. It is held at the beginning of May, with parades of chariots, participants are decorated with flowers using themes from the Greek mythology, tradition, nature etc. The event also includes, Folk Dancing and Singing. The festival is thought to originate in a celebration for Aphrodite.

CATAKLYSMOS

The festival is held 50 days after Easter on a Sunday at Kato Paphos Harbour. There are water games of various kinds and much eating, singing and dancing. Stalls offer various home made products. It is the celebration of the "Flood".

PAMPAPHIA

This is a new and well established folk festival which takes place during the first week of August. There are parades, bands (occasionally you may even enjoy the band of the Royal Highlanders). Greek folk singing and dancing, agricultural and art exhibitions and many gastronomic specialities, using the art of Cypriot cooking.

WINE FESTIVAL (DIONYSIA)

This is held during the last week of August or the first week of September at Stroumbi village, one of the Paphos wine centres. Local wine tasting and plentiful free wine are available. There is folk dancing, singing, and local food specialities. Also exhibitions of agricultural products, embroidery and lace are held.

OTHER FESTIVALS include the **AYIOS NEOPHITOS FARE** at the monastery, Sept. 27th & 28th; **ANCIENT DRAMA FESTIVAL** at the open ancient theatre (ODEON) with performances of ancient drama or comedies by students or theatrical groups during June-July; **APHRODITE FESTIVAL** organised by Paphos Beach and Annabelle Hotels with Fashion Shows, Exhibitions, Gastronomic evenings, Dances and a Contest for Miss Aphrodite-Paphos during July-August.

Other local festivals include: **LYSSOS VILLAGE** Festival **RESI** Festival at Kallepia, **Archaeological Symposium** at Kissonerga and Kouklia. Religious **FARE** (Panygiri) at Khrysorroyiatissa Mon.

Information about these and other festivals and accurate dates can be obtained from the Tourist Information Office in Paphos.

Two scenes from the Paphos Carnival.

Cypriot dancers during a local festival. *(Courtesy: Cyprus Tourism Organisation)*

Above: A Chariot decorated with flowers on Parade at the famous Paphos ANTHESTIRIA FESTIVAL.
(Courtesy Stephanos Theodorou) Below: Cypriot dancing. This is an exciting entertainment and is a feature
of most local festivals and special evening entertainments. The scene below is from PAMPAPHIA.

THE PAPHOS VILLAGE

This does not differ much from other Cypriot villages but due to its physical isolation has created some special characteristics.

The Village House: Two rooms, one next to the other, formed the traditional house. One room has a large bed for the parents and smaller for the children. In some places, up to 10 people could be accommodated. The room was also used as a sitting room. Next to it the kitchen with an open fire, storing space and a dining table. Poorer families had one long room only, richer families more rooms, some for their animals, and a few big landowners with their larger farmhouses.

Village Characteristics: Every village has a church and one or more **"Kafenia"** (the coffee-shops or village pubs) mainly situated in the village square, where all the males gather to sip their coffee or brandy, to gossip and play cards or backgammon. A couple of shops to sell different goods are the basic industries of a blacksmith and a cobbler. Sunday is a day for church and afterwards for social gathering. Wedding is the most important event of the village.

Local Panayiri (Fair): This occurs once or twice a year, mainly on the name day of the church saint. It starts with a pilgrimage to the saint, then a stroll around the fair to meet friends and buy local and other goods. It ends with a traditional feast of **souvla** (cooked meat on charcoal) or **"ofto"** (roast meat), with songs, dances, and drinking wine. This is a vital part of village life of religion, business and feasting.

The main village occupation is agriculture. In fertile lands, they grow wheat, barley, beans, potatoes, onions, vegetables, fruit. Livestock is very important to all villagers, each family has its own poultry and pigs, mules or donkeys. Some own cattle as well.

Emigration to cities and abroad has left many villages without young people and many schools are closed. Old traditions are slowly disappearing and the attractions of modern civilisation, as in other parts of the world are changing life.

A typical village house.

A typical village "kafenio"

THE VINEYARDS OF PAPHOS

Vineyards in Paphos are as old as its history. They were and still are the backbone of the economy of the district and villagers take much pride of their product.

But the cultivation of vineyards until recently was done in primitive ways and reaching the various vineyards on the slopes of the hills was difficult. However, existing truck roads are now wide and other special truck roads have been constructed.

Grants were given to the villagers and new vineyards were planned with better table grapes and better wine producing grapes. The cultivation is also done in a professional way, thus increasing production.

In the months of late July, August and early September, the countryside is full of people collecting the grapes, transporting them from the vineyards into baskets on the back of donkeys to the lorries which then transport them to the wineries. Some of the grape juice is spilled on the roads making them slippery, thus take care when driving.

The main winery in Paphos is that of SODAP at Ayios Antonios Street, between Aloe Hotel and Rania Apartments. The major wineries including that of KEO are in Limassol.

Above: Collecting grapes; Right: View of vineyards
(Courtesy: Cyprus Trade Centre — London)

PAPHOS PRODUCTIVE TREES

CARROB TREES

OLIVE TREES

CARROB TREES

This is a rare survivor of the iron age. They grow in the countryside and require the minimum of care. Once they were called "the Black Gold" of Cyprus and were exported in great quantities from the harbour of Paphos mainly as animal feed. Carrobs also produce tasty honey.

OLIVE TREES

This is a sacred tree to the Greek world. In Paphos it grows wild but also under supervision in fields. Both oil and olives are mainly consumed locally and form a main item of Cypriot diet.

Carrob fruit

BANANAS

These are extensively grown in the Paphos district, are small but of excellent quality. The biggest enemy is frost which is rare in Paphos but great precaution is taken during winter. The banana trees require much care and lots of water. They are consumed in the island and also exported mainly to Arab countries.

ORANGES

LEMONS

CITRUS TREES

Orange and Lemon production in Paphos has been expanded since the Turkish invasion and the occupation of the citrus growing areas of Morphou and Famagusta. The numerous dams erected in the Paphos district provide much needed water. Both lemons and oranges are of excellent quality and some are exported to British and other markets.

ALMOND TREES

These are widely grown in most parts of the district and in many other parts of the island and due to the local and International demand of Almond Nuts, the product gives a reasonable revenue without requiring much attention.

The Almond trees are also liked for their blossoms during the spring, a sheer delight of beauty expressed by many poets and painted by many artists.

ALMOND TREES   ALMOND TREE BLOSSOMS

THE WEATHER

Average max. day temperatures in Paphos (° Farenheit)

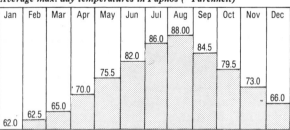

Jan	Feb	Mar	Apr	May	Jun	Jul	Aug	Sep	Oct	Nov	Dec
62.0	62.5	65.0	70.0	75.5	82.0	86.0	88.00	84.5	79.5	73.0	66.0

General climate: Paphos, surrounded on three sides by the sea has the mildest climate in Cyprus, where the summer heat is cooled with the breeze from the sea and the winters are fairly mild. However rain falls from time to time in the spring so do not be surprised if you find a few days of rain or bad weather in February or March even in April, although this is not regular and predictable.

Early spring provides natural excitement with green fields wild flowers, trees of oranges, lemon almond in blossom and others with their extraordinary beauty Migrating birds like swallows arrive and the whole countryside is completely different to that of the dry summer.

What to wear. From October to the end of March it is advisable to take some thicker clothes and cardigans as well as it gets cold especially during the night when the sun has gone. During the winter months, when the wind blows from the north, it can get very cold. But in the summer light clothing and a thin cardigan for the night is all that is necessary as it is very hot.

MEDICAL CARE

It is always an upsetting experience when any visitor becomes unwell and needs medical attention. Medicine in most countries, not excluding Cyprus, is private and the visitor has to pay for services rendered though charges are low, ranging from £5 - £10 for a visit at the doctor's surgery. Charges for home visits are a little higher and depend on the amount of medical treatment given. In any case, these charges should not exceed £20 for a visit within the town limits. One can find medical care in most branches of medicine, though not all doctors are English speaking. There are, in the town, British qualified specialists and these are probably the best to seek advice from bearing in mind the colloquial way in which the British express themselves. Their standard is amongst the highest on the island, in medicine and surgery.

The hospital service is government run and care is paid for by visitors. Private clinics offer a better standard of nursing care

Paphos Countryside is beter seen during the Spring when the countryside is green and flowers are everywhere, a real paradise.

ACCOMMODATION

Accommodation in Paphos caters for all pockets and all requirements. All officially rated accommodation by the Cyprus Tourism Organisation is listed below as published in 1989. Many other hotels and apartments are under construction.

HOTEL ACCOMMODATION

			Tel. (06)
ALEXANDER THE GREAT	★★★★	Posidonos Ave.	237928
ANNABELLE	★★★★	Posidonos Ave.	238333
CYPRIA MARIS	★★★★	Posidonos Ave.	238111
IMPERIAL BEACH	★★★★	Posidonos Ave.	—
LEDRA BEACH	★★★★	Posidonos Ave.	243373
PAPHOS BEACH	★★★★	Posidonos Ave.	233091
ALOE	★★★	Posidonos Ave.	234000
AVLIDA	★★★	Tombs of Kings Area	
CYNTHIANA BEACH	★★★	Kissonerga	233900
DIONYSOS	★★★	2 Dionysiou St.	233414
KISSOS	★★★	Tombs of Kings Rd	236111
MELINA	★★★	Ay. Lambrianos St.	244400
NEREUS SUNOTEL	★★★	Constantia St.	243101
PAPHIANA	★★★	Konia/Yeroskipos	235252
PAPHIAN BAY	★★★	Posidonos St.	243333
PORTO PAPHOS	★★★	Posidonos St.	242333
THEOFANO	★★★	Danaes St.	233666
VERONICA	★★★	Danaes St.	236333
APOLLO	★★	St. Paul Ave.	233909
AXIOTHEA	★★	Hebes Malioti St.	232866
KINGS	★★	Tombs of Kings Rd	233497
NEW OLYMPUS	★★	12 Byron St.	232020
AGAPINOR	★	24 St. Paul Ave.	233926
PYRAMOS	★	Ay. Anastasias St.	235161

PAPHOS DISTRICT

MARION	★★	Polis Town
G & P LATCHI	★★	Latchi — Polis
SOULI	★	Neokhorio Village
YERONISSOS	★	Ayios Yeoryios Peyias
TYLO BEACH	★	Kato Pyrgos
AYII ANARGYRI	★	Miliou Village

APARTMENT ACCOMMODATION

	Class		Tel. (06)
DAPHNE	— A —	3 Alkminis St.	233500
DEMETRA	— A —	Artemidos St.	234444
HELIOS BAY	— A —	Khlorakas	235656
RANIA	— A —	Posidonos Ave.	235444
SOFIANNA	— A —	Agamemnou St	235111
EURONEST	— B —	Coral Bay	(066) 21121
HILLTOP GARDENS	— B —	Tombs of Kings Rd	243111
MIROFORI	— B —	Constantias St.	234311
PANDREAM	— B —	Polydefkis St.	236401
RODOTHEA	— B —	Ay. Antonios St.	238719
THESEAS	— B —	1-3 Iasonos St.	235511
ALOMA	— C —	Klytemnistra	237400
AMBASSADOR	— C —	Hebes Malioti St.	235440
LAND OF KINGS	— C —	Tombs of Kings Rd	241770
PAPHOS GARDENS	— C —	P.o. Box 195	234041
BASILICA GARDENS	-New-	Near Harbour P.O. Box 195	
ANEMI APARTMENTS	-New-	Near Posidonos Ave.	

PAPHOS DISTRICT

ELIAS	— A —	Latchi-Polis
FOLLOW THE SUN	— B —	Polis
NICOS & OLYMPIA	— B —	Polis
DROUSIA HEIGHTS	— A —	Droushia Village
KAMARES VILLAGE	— B —	Tala P.O. Box 195
STEPHANIE VILLAGE	— B —	Tala P.O. Box 195
CORALENIA		Coral Bay

CAMPING

ZENON GARDENS	Yeroskipos	233192
POLIS CAMPING	Polis (063)	32351

OTHER ACCOMMODATION

There are private individuals who let their houses or apartments in estate complexes. This is arranged directly with the owners or their agents, but you should take care since overcharging or poor accommodation could create problems. **Monasteries;** provide overnight or short stay accommodation without charge, a voluntary contribution towards the monastery is advisable. During the busy summer months it is better to check for availability due to the large number of tourists. Accommodation also is provided at **Stavros tis Psokas** forest station. Please phone (021) 40 2264 or contact the Forestry Office at Nicosia (074) 17454 for reservations.

CAMPING There is a well organised camping site between Polis and the sea, close to the beach. There are toilets, showers, cooking and washing facilities, cafeteria and supermarket.

Provisional permission has been given to a limited number of restaurant owners to operate a camp site near their establishment which provide the basic needs. They include the area around the Baths of Aphrodite and Keratidhi at Coral Bay.

YOUTH HOSTELS

Paphos has a youth hostel which is situated to the north east part of the town and offers accommodation mainly to members of the **International Youth Hostels Association.** The address is 37 Eleftherios Venizelos Avenue, Paphos tel 21588 or 32588.

At Stavros tis Psokas, in the centre of Paphos forest, there is a small hostel with 12 beds.

For both hostels contact:
Cyprus Youth Hostels Assoc.
P.O. Box 1328 — Nicosia.

ALL HOTELS & APARTMENTS

★ Provide laundry and dry-cleaning facilities, mainly contracted to an outside company and you pay accordingly.

★ All hotels have shops providing essential items, souvenirs, books, some have hairdressing and other facilities. Apartments supply basic provisions for cooking.

★ Many establishments provide evening entertainment.

★ You are free to go to any establishment to drink at the bar or the cafeteria, eat at the restaurant or enquire about their special evenings.

PUBLIC BUILDINGS & SERVICES

POST OFFICE.
The main office providing all postal services including new issues for stamp collectors is situated at Nikodimou Milona St. Opening hours Mon-Fri, 7.30am-1.30pm and 3.30pm-5.30pm. Early closing Wed. Sat 7.30am-12.30pm.

Post office boxes can be obtained. Other small branches exist in other parts of the town, at Polis and some major villages.

POLICE STATION.
This is situated in Kennedy Square and close to 28th October Square. It is the headquarters of the Paphos district and its buildings resemble old colonial architecture. Officers will be glad to assist you with any problems you may have. Call 199 for emergencies or 32352 for general information.

GENERAL HOSPITAL.
This is situated at Neophytou Nicolaidi Ave., Tel 32364 and is part of Cyprus' Free Medical Care. Visitors to Paphos can visit the hospital should they have any problems (see also under Medical Care).

TOWN HALL.
Situated to the east of 28th October Square where events and exhibitions take place at certain times.

TELEGRAPHIC OFFICE/ TELECOMMU-NICATIONS.
Situated at Georgiou Griva Dhigeni Ave and can connect you with any part of the world.

Direct TELEPHONE Connections exist with many countries. Most operators speak English and will help with any enquiries. Dial 192. The telephone directory is printed in both Greek and English.

To dial direct: Athens-00301, London-00441, Paris-00331, Bonn-00492228, New York-001212, Rome-00396.

Inland Dial codes: Paphos-061 (from outside Paphos), Nicosia-021, Limassol-051, Larnaca-041, Ayia Napa 046, Paralimni-031.

PUBLIC LIBRARY.
Situated to the west of 28th October square. This small library has a considerable number of books in Greek but also in English and a few in French. Lending facilities are available. Another library also operates on a lending basis, that of the Anglo-American school (22-26 Hellas Ave). Opening hours: Tue & Fri 10.00am-12.30pm/2.30pm-4.30pm, Wed 2.30pm-4.30pm.

THE SCHOOLS.
These buildings are in Grecian style to the north of 28th October Sq. and George Grivas Dhigenis Ave and house an elementary school, an economics higher education school and the Gymnasium where in it's large hall, concerts, plays and lectures take place. Behind is the old stadium where track field activities and football take place except during the summer days when its too hot.

COURTS/DISTRICT ADMINISTRATION.
These buildings are situated at Nicodimou Milonas St. close to the general post office and are of British colonial architectural style.

USEFUL TELEPHONES

Paphos Code (06)

Town Hall & Services	232116
District Court	232482
Agricultural Dept.	232064
Fisheries Department	232192
Handicraft Shop	232300
District Governor	232143
Police Headquarters	232352
Harbour Police	233988
Fire Service	232294
Customs Office	232008
Central Post Office	232241
District Archaeological Dept. & Museum	232554
General Hospital	232364
Cyprus Airways	236941
Paphos Airport	236120
Airport Customs	236832

MONEY MATTERS

As from October 1983 a new currency was introduced to replace the old decimal monetary system. The new currency is the **CENT.** The unit of currency is the Cyprus Pound CY£ and is divided into 100 cent (previously 1000 mils). New coins have been introduced which are: ½ cent (5 mils), 1 cent (10 mils), 2 cent (20 mils), 5 cent (50 mils), 10 cent (100 mils), and 20 cent. Those in brackets are the corresponding old values.

Bank notes remain the same and will be gradually replaced by the new values. They are (250 mils) new 25 cent, (500 mils) new 50 cent, CY£1 and the new CY£5 and CY£10.

The main banking business and dealings are done by the Central Bank of Cyprus which will give advice on any monetary enquiries which you may have: Central Bank of Cyprus, 36 Metochiou Street, P.O. Box 1087, Nicosia, Tel 45281.

All your banking business and exchange of money can be done in one of the following banks which have main offices in Paphos (Ktima) main shopping area and also have smaller branches at Kato Paphos and Polis.

They are: Bank of Cyprus; Popular Bank (Laiki); Hellenic Bank; Co-Operative Bank; Barclays Bank; National Bank of Greece; Lombard Bank.

Banks open daily Mon-Sat 8.30am to 12 noon. Exchange of travellers cheques can be done by hotels and large shops. You may bring in as much foreign currency as you want but on departing you are not allowed to take any currency over a certain sum which at present is about £40, although unchanged travellers cheques are no problem, so do not exchange more of your travellers cheques than is necessary.

The two main Cyprus banks have head offices and branches in London.
Bank of Cyprus (London) Ltd. 27-31 Charlotte Street, London W1P 4BH.
Cyprus Popular Bank: 23 Fitzroy Street, London W1P 6BA.

PUBLIC HOLIDAYS

Some of the holidays are observed Nationally, others by educational or civil service or by the public.

January: 1st-New Year; 6th-Epiphane; 19th-Name day of Archbishop Makarios.
Good Friday/Easter Saturday-Sunday-Monday.
March 25th-Greek National Day.
April 1st-Cyprus National Day.
May 1st-Labour Day.
August 3rd-Anniversary of Death of Archbishop Makarios.
October 1st-Independence Day; 28th-Greek National Day.
December 24, 25th, 26th, CHRISTMAS.

OPENING HOURS OF PUBLIC PLACES

Opening hours vary according to the season and you may get up to date times from the tourist Office. Museums and archaeological sites usually open: Mon-Fri 7.30am-5.00pm; Sat. 7.30am-5.00pm; Sun. 10.00am-1.00pm (museum only).
Some places close for one or two hours for lunch. Winter times are shorter.

MONASTERIES

These Monasteries have been described in the excursions section and they are: Ayios Neophitos and Khrysorroyiatissa. Please note the following.
- Accommodation is offered in both for a limited number of nights
- A small donation to the Church is always welcome
- The monasteries are included in organised tours.
- Visitors, especially women are advised to avoid wearing short trousers and to be dressed decently.
- During Sundays and after the morning service, Christenings usually take place and visitors are welcome to watch.
- Paniyiri (Religious fares) take place: at Ayios Neophitos:— Jan. 23-24 and Sept. 27-28. at Khrysorroyiatissa: Feb 1-2 and August 14-15.

ENGLISH LANGUAGE NEWSPAPERS

There is a daily English language paper called **"Cyprus Mail"** and a much larger weekly called **"Cyprus Weekly"** both providing local, British and International news, local radio and TV programmes, festivals, events, sports, art and eating places. National British newspapers can also be found at certain places.

RADIO AND TELEVISION

The Cyprus Broadcasting Corporation (telephone Nicosia 22231) provides daily radio and television services in Greek, with special programmes in Turkish, English, Armenian and French. Special tourist broadcasts are made during the summer time mainly in English, German and French. For times please consult your hotel or look into the Cyprus Mail or Cyprus Weekly for details.

Do not be surprised if you tune into an English language radio station: this is the BFBS (British Forces Broadcasting Service — Cyprus) and broadcasts in English daily on medium wave and VHF. Details of daily programmes can be found in the Cyprus Mail.

DIPLOMATIC MISSIONS

All Diplomatic Missions are based in Nicosia, the capital of the island. They include:

UK HIGH COMMISSION – Alexander Pallis St. (02) 473131
FRENCH EMBASSY – 6 Ploutarchos St. Engomi (02) 465258
WEST GERMAN EMBASSY – Ionikitaras St. (02) 444362
GREEK EMBASSY – 8-10 Byron Avenue (02) 441880
ITALIAN EMBASSY – 5 Dinokratou St. (02) 473183
U.S.A. EMBASSY – Theorissou St. (02) 465151
UNFCYP – Headquarters (02) 464000

PLEASE REMEMBER . . .

Antiquities are important to Cyprus' culture. Therefore it is absolutely forbidden to export any kind of archaeological items, whether large or small, without proper permission obtained from the Director of the Department of Antiquities in Nicosia.
It is also illegal to remove any antiquities or stones from archaeological sites or the sea bed.

PAPHOS, A PLACE TO RETIRE

Paphos, from all other places in the island, is the most popular place to retire and settle. The place has already attracted a large number of people, mainly British who have settled and bought their own home or apartment either by the sea, around Coral Bay or in the villages above Paphos with their commanding panoramic views.

Others have bought a holiday home which they use for their holidays and also rent it out to other tourists.
Paphos has been chosen as an ideal place for retirement due to the mild climate, the beautiful landscapes, variety of excellent and inexpensive food, wines and brandies and the traditional friendliness and hospitality of its people.
The British community now amounts to a considerable number and they have formed their own association.

For those wishing to purchase a flat or a house or to make Paphos as their permanent place of residence, contact one of the specialist developers who will arrange it for you or the Cyprus Tourism Organisation who will advise you where to apply.

When responding to any advertisements, please mention " Paphos–Land of Aphrodite"

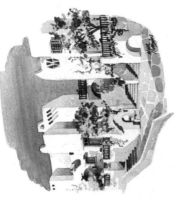

Ikaria *village* Paphos

YOU FEEL SECURE WITH US

The latest CONTRACTA development in traditional Greek Island architecture

- Beautifully landscaped, with a village square, paved pathways, fountains, gardens, swimming pool, shops, restaurants, an artificial lake and a small Byzantine church.

- Villas, villa type apartments and maisonettes, with large verandahs, private gardens and parking, ideal for residence, retirement or vacations.

LORDOS CONTRACTA
GEORGE D. LORDOS & SONS LTD.
P.O.BOX 1175 LIMASSOL – CYPRUS TEL. 77977 TELEX 5136

CONTRACTA
LORDOS

107

ELIA
HOTEL
APARTMENTS

LATSI-POLIS
Tel. (063) 21011
(Latsi)
Telex: 4420 DESO CY

A small luxury complex consisting of 28 fully furnished apartments all having a beautiful view to the sea. There are studios, one and two bedroom apartments — all one bedroom apts are two-storied i.e. *(downstairs living room, kitchen and upstairs bedroom and bathroom/wc).*

There is also a bar, swimming pool, tennis court, playground, landscaping, mini market, and water sports facilities can be arranged at the reception.

This complex is designed and built for individuals and families wishing to enjoy a holiday away from the crowds in an unspoilt area. Situated 50 meters from the sea nd 100 meters from Latsi fishing harbour with its fish tavernas offering fresh sea-food and excellent wines. The historic Aphrodite Baths are only a short distance.

When responding to any advertisements, please mention " Paphos-Land of Aphrodite"

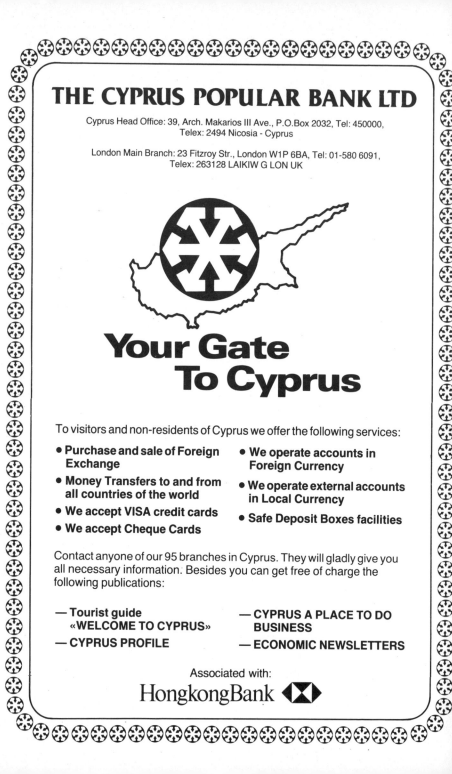